Walter Debenham Sweeting

The Cathedral Church of Peterborough

A description of its fabric and a brief history of the episcopal see

Walter Debenham Sweeting

The Cathedral Church of Peterborough
A description of its fabric and a brief history of the episcopal see

ISBN/EAN: 9783337259600

Printed in Europe, USA, Canada, Australia, Japan

Cover: Foto ©Lupo / pixelio.de

More available books at **www.hansebooks.com**

CATHEDRAL SERIES:
D BY GLEESON WHITE
EDWARD F. STRANGE

PETERBOROUGH

Photochrom Co., Ltd. Photo. PETERBOROUGH CATHEDRAL, FROM THE SOUTH-EAST.

THE CATHEDRAL CHURCH OF
PETERBOROUGH

A DESCRIPTION OF ITS FABRIC AND A BRIEF HISTORY OF THE EPISCOPAL SEE

BY

THE REV. W. D. SWEETING, M.A.

LONDON
GEORGE BELL & SONS
1898

GENERAL PREFACE.

This series of monographs has been planned to supply visitors to the great English Cathedrals with accurate and well illustrated guide-books at a popular price. The aim of each writer has been to produce a work compiled with sufficient knowledge and scholarship to be of value to the student of Archæology and History, and yet not too technical in language for the use of an ordinary visitor or tourist.

To specify all the authorities which have been made use of in each case would be difficult and tedious in this place. But amongst the general sources of information which have been almost invariably found useful are : — (1) the great county histories, the value of which, especially in questions of genealogy and local records, is generally recognised ; (2) the numerous papers by experts which appear from time to time in the Transactions of the Antiquarian and Archæological Societies ; (3) the important documents made accessible in the series issued by the Master of the Rolls ; (4) the well-known works of Britton and Willis on the English Cathedrals ; and (5) the very excellent series of Handbooks to the Cathedrals, originated by the late Mr. John Murray, to which the reader may in most cases be referred for fuller detail, especially in reference to the histories of the respective sees.

GLEESON WHITE.
E. F. STRANGE.
Editors of the Series.

AUTHOR'S PREFACE.

THE chief authorities consulted in the preparation of this book are named in the text. Besides the well-known works mentioned in the General Preface, and the "Monastic Chronicles," there are several that deal with Peterborough alone, of which the most important and valuable are "Gunton's History" with Dean Patrick's Supplement, "Craddock's History," the monographs by Professor Paley and Mr Poole, and the Guide of Canon Davys. If I have ventured to differ from some of these writers on various points, I must appeal, in justification, to a careful and painstaking study of the Cathedral and its history, during a residence at Peterborough of more than twenty years.

My best thanks are due to Mr Caster of Peterborough, for permission to incorporate with this account the substance of a Guide, which I prepared for him, published in 1893; and to Mr Robert Davison of London, for his description of the Mosaic Pavement, executed by him for the Choir. I desire also to express my thanks for the drawings supplied by Mr W. H. Lord, Mr H. P. Clifford, and Mr O. R. Allbrow; and to acknowledge my indebtedness to the Photochrom Company, Ld., and to Messrs S. B. Bolas & Co., for their excellent photographs.

W. D. SWEETING.

CONTENTS.

	PAGE
CHAPTER I.—History of the Cathedral Church of S. Peter	3
CHAPTER II.—The Cathedral—Exterior	36
The West Front	39
The Towers	44
The Porch and Parvise	45
The Bell-Tower	48
The Dean's Door	50
The Lantern-Tower	51
The North Transept	52
The New Building	55
The South Transept	55
CHAPTER III.—The Cathedral—Interior	57
The Choir	60
The Choir Stalls	67
The Pulpit and Throne	70
The Organ, Baldachino, and Pavement	72
The Screens	74
The Lectern	74
The New Building	76
The Transepts	77
The Saxon Church	80
The Nave	81
The Nave Ceiling	84
The West Transept	87
Altars	87
Stained Glass	88
The Parvise	90
Monuments and Inscriptions	91
CHAPTER IV.—The Minster Precincts and City	99
The Chapel of S. Thomas of Canterbury	100
The Knights' Chamber	101
The Deanery Gateway	102
The Infirmary and Cloisters	103
The Palace	106
The City and Guild Hall	108
The Tithe Barn	111
CHAPTER V.—History of the Monastery	112
CHAPTER VI.—History of the Diocese	127

ILLUSTRATIONS.

	PAGE
The Cathedral, from the South-East	*Frontispiece*
Arms of the Diocese	*Title*
The Cathedral and Palace	2
The Cathedral, from the North, c. 1730	7
Remains of Saxon Church	9
Map, 1610	23
The West Front in the Seventeenth Century	25
Iron Railings, 1721	27
Finial of the Central Gable of the West Front	34
The West Front	37
Plan of Central Portion of the West Front	41
West Porch and Parvise	43
Gates to West Porch	44
South-West Spire and Bell-Tower	47
The West Front, restored according to Gunton, 1780	49
The Dean's Door	51
Apse and New Building, from the South-East	53
Plan of Monastery Buildings	58
The Choir	61
View from the Triforium South of Choir	63
North Transept and Morning Chapel	65
The Pulpit	71
Apse and Canopied Reredos	73
The New Building—Interior	78
The Transepts, looking North	79
Evangelistic Symbols, from Lantern Tower Roof	80, 81
Boss from Lantern Tower Roof	82
The Nave, looking East	83
The Choir and Nave, looking West	85
Head of S. Peter in Ancient Stained Glass	89
Part of the Monks' Stone	92
Saxon Coffin Lids in North Transept	93
Portions of Abbots' Tombs	94, 95, 96
South Aisles of Choir and Nave	97
South Side of the Close, 1801	99
Cathedral Gateway, 1791	101
Door to Palace Grounds from the Cloisters, 1797	104
Door way to Cathedral from the Cloisters	105
Archway from Cloisters, North-West	107
Church of S. John the Baptist and Guildhall	109
Rose Windows and Details of West Front	117
Tomb of an Abbot, possibly Abbot Andrew, 1201	120
Iron Railings, 1721	123
Details of Chasubles on Abbots' Tombs	129, 133
PLAN OF THE CATHEDRAL	135

Photochrom Co., Ld., Photo.

THE CATHEDRAL AND PALACE, FROM THE SOUTH-WEST.

PETERBOROUGH CATHEDRAL.

CHAPTER I.

HISTORY OF THE CATHEDRAL CHURCH OF S. PETER.

UNTIL some fifty years ago, Peterborough remained one of the most perfect and unchanged examples in the kingdom of the monastic borough. The place was called into existence by the monastery and was entirely dependent on it. The Abbot was supreme lord, and had his own gaol. He possessed great power over the whole hundred. And even after the See of Peterborough was constituted, and the Abbey Church became a cathedral, many of the ancient privileges were retained by the newly formed Dean and Chapter. They still retained the proclamation and control of the fairs; their officer, the high bailiff, was the returning officer at elections for parliament; they regulated the markets; they appointed the coroner. Professor Freeman contrasts an Abbot's town with a Bishop's town, when speaking about the city of Wells.[1] "An Abbot's borough might arise anywhere; no better instance can be found than the borough of S. Peter itself, that Golden Borough which often came to be called distinctively the Borough without further epithet." And again, "the settlement which arose around the great fenland monastery of S. Peter, the holy house of Medeshampstead, grew by degrees into a borough, and by later ecclesiastical arrangements, into a city, a city and borough to which the changes of our own day have given a growth such as it never knew before."

Situated on the edge of the Fens, some miles to the east of the great north road, without any special trade, and without any

---

[1] "English Towns and Districts," 1883, pp. 103, 130.

neighbouring territorial magnates, it is hardly surprising that the place seemed incapable of progress, and remained long eminently respectable and stagnant. In one of his caustic epigrams Dean Duport does indeed speak of the wool-combers as if there were a recognised calling that employed some numbers of men; but he is not complimentary to those employed, for he says that the men that comb the wool, and the sheep that bear it, are on a par as regards intelligence :

> "At vos simplicitate pares et moribus estis,
> Lanificique homines, lanigerique greges."

In another epigram he derides the city itself, calling it contemptuously "Urbicula": and he suggests, with a humour that to modern ideas savours of irreverence, that this little city of S. Peter's, "Petropolis," unless S. Peter had the keys, would run away through its own gates.

The great development of the last half century is due to the railway works at New England, and to the Great Northern Line making Peterborough an important railway centre. In 1807 the entire population of the city and hamlets was under 3500. In 1843 it was just over 5500, and when the railway was laid it was not much more than 6000. It has since gone up by leaps and bounds. In 1861 the population exceeded 11,000: in 1871, 15,200; in 1881, 19,300; and in 1891, 23,600. The private diary of a resident of less than forty years ago, would read like an old world record. The watchman in the Minster Precincts still went his rounds at night and called out the time and the weather; sedan-chairs were in use; the corn-market of the neighbourhood was held in the open street; turnpikes took toll at every road out of the town; a weekly paper had only just been started on a humble scale, being at first little more than a railway time-table with a few items of local news at the back; a couple of rooms more than sufficed for the business of the post office.

In 1874 a charter of incorporation was granted, not without some opposition; it had been, up to that time, the only city in England without a mayor.

An account of the church which is now the cathedral church of a diocese that was only constituted in 1541, must of necessity trace its history for some centuries before it attained its present dignity, and when it was simply the church of an abbey.

Three centuries and a half of cathedral dignity have not made its old name of Minster obsolete; it is indeed the term usually employed.[1]

The village was first known by the name of Medeshamstede, the homestead in the meadows. There is no evidence that any houses were built at all before the foundation of the monastery. There was probably not a single habitation on the spot before the rising walls of the religious house made dwelling-places for the workmen a necessity. As time went on the requirements of the inmates brought together a population, which for centuries had no interests unconnected with the abbey. The establishment of the monastery is due to the conversion of the royal family to Christianity. It was in the middle of the seventh century when Penda was King of the Mercians, and his children, three sons, Peada, Wulfere, and Ethelred, and two daughters, Kyneburga, and Kyneswitha, became converted to the Christian faith. On succeeding to the throne, Peada the eldest son, founded this monastery of Medeshamstede. The first Abbot, Saxulf, had been in a high position at court; he is described as an earl (*comes*); and most likely had the practical duty of building and organising the monastery, as he is called by Bede the builder of the place as well as first Abbot (*Constructor et abbas*). This was in the year 654 or 655 (for the date is given differently by different authorities), and Peada only lived two or three years afterwards. His brothers in turn came to the throne, and both helped to enrich the rising foundation. The elder of the two, however, had lapsed from Christianity, and killed his own two sons in his rage at finding they had become Christians; but afterwards stung with remorse he confessed his offence to S. Chad, who had brought the princes to the knowledge of Christ, and offered to expiate it in any way he was directed. He was bidden to restore the Christian Religion, to repair the ruined churches, and to found new ones. The whole story is told with great particularity by the chronicler, and it was represented in stained glass in the cloisters of the abbey, as described hereafter.

[1] A few other cathedrals which were originally churches of monasteries are still called Minsters, as York (nearly always), Canterbury (occasionally), Ripon, Southwell, and perhaps more. Lincoln Cathedral though often called a Minster was a Cathedral from the first, and was never attached to a monastery.

The church thus built must have been of considerable substance, if, as recorded, Peada in the foundation of it " laid such stones as that eight yoke of oxen could scarce draw one of them."[1] It has nevertheless, utterly perished. We read of the continued support bestowed by a succession of princes and nobles, of the increasing dignity of the house, and of the privileges it acquired ; but there is nowhere a single line descriptive of the buildings themselves. Gunton does indeed speak of a goodly house for the Abbot constructed by King Peada ; but he must have been capable of strange credulity if he imagined, as his words seem to imply, that this very house was in existence in the time of Henry VIII. He writes thus : [1] "The Royal Founder . . . built also an house for the Abbot, which upon the dissolution by Henry the Eighth, became the Bishop's Palace. A building very large and stately, as the present age can testifie ; all the rooms of common habitation being built above stairs, and underneath are very fair vaults and goodly cellars for several uses. The great Hall, a magnificent room, had, at the upper end, in the Wall, very high above the ground, three stately Thrones, wherein were placed sitting, the three Royal Founders carved curiously of Wood, painted and guilt, which in the year 1644 were pulled down and broken to pieces."

There is no doubt that this first monastery was utterly destroyed by the Danes about the year 870. The very circumstantial account given in the chronicle of Abbot John, derived from Ingulf, is well known ; but as it is entirely without corroboration in any of the historians who mention the destruction of the monastery, recent criticism has not hesitated to pronounce the whole account a mere invention. It is unnecessary, therefore, to give it here. The account "may have some foundation in fact," Professor Freeman admits, "but if so. it is strange to find no mention of it in Orderic."[2] But the discredit thrown upon the minutely graphic story of Ingulf, does not of course apply to the actual fact, of which there is ample evidence, that the monastery was burnt by the Danes. Matthew of Westminster says :[3] —"And so the wicked

---

[1] Gunton, p. 4.
[2] "Ingulf and the Historia Croylandensis." By W. G. Searle, M.A., Camb. Antiq. Soc., 8vo. xxvii. p. 65.
[3] Searle : Ingulf, p. 63.

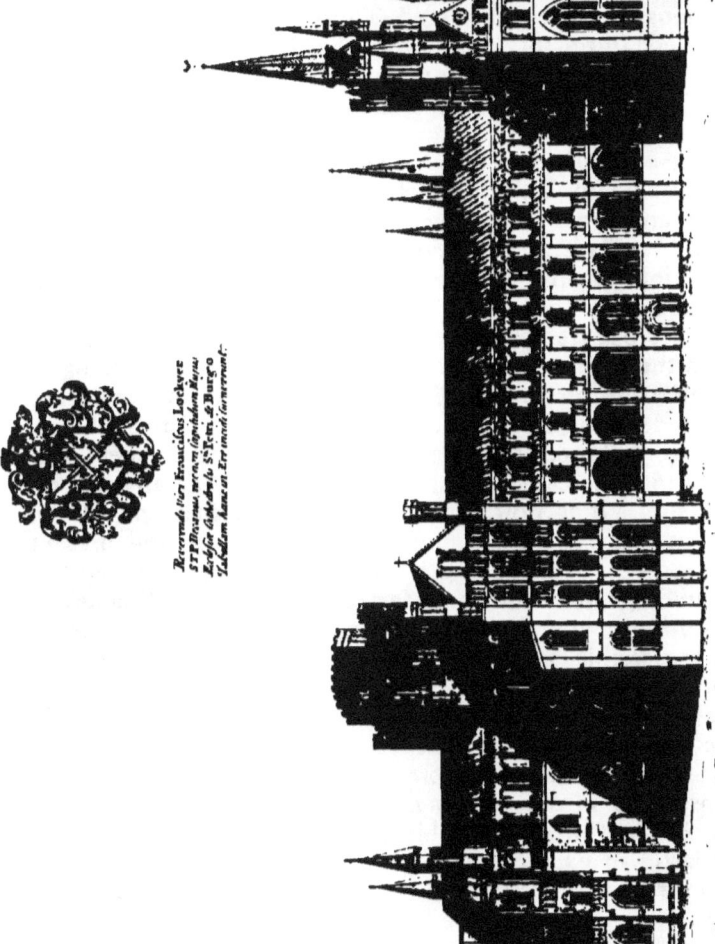

NORTH SIDE OF THE CATHEDRAL.

leaders, passing through the district of York, burned the churches, cities, and villages . . . and thence advancing they destroyed all the monasteries (*cœnobia*) of monks and nuns situated in the fens, and slew the inmates. The names of these monasteries are, Crowland, Thorney, Ramsey, Hamstede, now called Burgh S. Peter, with the Isle of Ely, and that once very famous house of nuns, wherein the holy Virgin and Queen Etheldreda laudably discharged the office of abbess for many years."

The re-edification of the monastery, henceforth known as Burgh, is due to Bishop Ethelwold, of Winchester, with the approval and support of King Edgar. This was accomplished in 972. We have now reached a point where all can take a practical interest in the subject, because portions of this church are to be seen to this day. The exact site of the Saxon church had always been a matter of conjecture until the excavations made in the course of the works incidental to the rebuilding of the lantern tower (1883–1893) finally settled the question. Many students of the fabric supposed that the existing church practically followed the main outlines of the former one, possibly with increased length and breadth, but at any rate on the old site. It is now ascertained that the east end of the Saxon church was nearly under the east wall of the present south transept, and the south walls of the south transepts of both buildings were but a very few feet apart. The dimensions of the former church, both its length and breadth, were as nearly as possible half of those of the existing one. A description of the present appearance of the remains will be found in a later chapter.

The Church of Bishop Ethelwold was not without its vicissitudes. Nothing was more promising than its origin, and the circumstances of its building. King Edgar and Dunstan, whom he had made Archbishop of Canterbury, were very enthusiastic in extending the growth of monastic influence in the country. No less than forty Benedictine convents are said to have been either founded or restored by Edgar. Bishop Ethelwold was entirely of one mind with the King and Archbishop, in the ecclesiastical reforms of the day. Mr Poole well describes the commencement of the work. "At Medeshamstede the ruins were made to their hands, and they at once commenced the grateful task of their restoration and appropriation. As usual, we find certain supernatural interferences assigned as indications of the divine approval of the work. It is related how Ethelwold was directed by God, in a dream, to go to the monastery of S. Peter, among the Mid-English; how he halted first at Oundle, supposing that to be

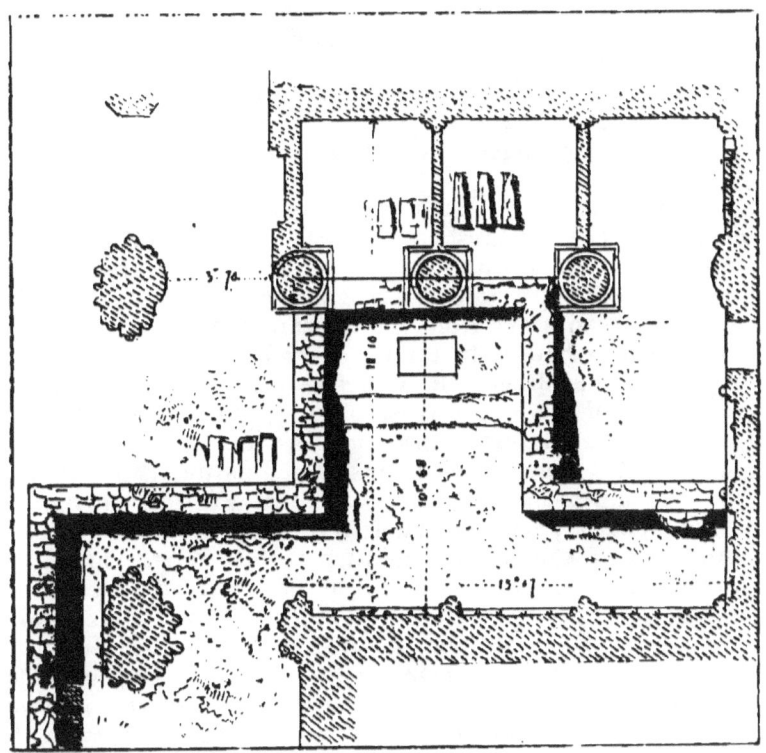

REMAINS OF SAXON CHURCH (THE PIERS AND WALLS OF PRESENT SOUTH TRANSEPT SHADED DIAGONALLY). DRAWN BY W. H. LORD.

the monastery intended; but being warned in a dream to continue his eastward course, at length discovered the ashes of the desolated Medeshamstede. It needs but little ingenuity to collect from this that Ethelwold, having received some vague intelligence of the present condition both of Oundle and Medeshamstede, started from Winchester, determined on reaching either or both; and that being less pleased with what he saw at Oundle than he expected, he extended his progress to Medeshamstede."[1] The Queen is said to have overheard the Bishop's fervent prayers for the success of his object, and to have used her influence with the King; but he probably required very little persuasion to undertake what was so much to his taste. It may be mentioned that if we accept the date 972 for the completion of the re-building (the Chronicle gives 970 for its commencement), the very same year witnessed that well-known scene on the River Dee, when King Edgar held the helm of a royal barge as it was being rowed by eight vassal kings.

The King came to visit the monastery thus rebuilt under his direction. The Archbishops, Dunstan and Oswald, with a large company of the nobility and clergy attended at the same time. The King is said to have inspected some old deeds which had been saved from the general destruction a century before, and to have wept for joy at reading the privileges belonging to the place. He therefore granted a new charter, confirming all the old privileges and possessions. Since in this charter no allusion is made to the triple dedication of the church, but S. Peter alone seems named as the Patron Saint, it is not unreasonable to conclude that the first church of Burgh monastery was dedicated to S. Peter only, and that the dedication of the original minster to SS. Peter, Paul, and Andrew, was not repeated. Edgar says that he renews the ancient privileges "*pro gratia Sancti Petri*"; and that certain immunities shall continue as long as the Abbot and the inmates of the house remain in the peace of God, and the Patron Saint continues his protection, "*ipso Abbate cum subjecta Christi familia in pace Dei, et superni Janitoris Petro patrocinio illud (sc. cœnobium) regente.*" This charter is noteworthy for the title the King gives himself, "*Ego Edgar totius Albionis Basileus.*"

For some time this establishment continued to flourish. But the troublous times that followed the Norman conquest did not leave Burgh undamaged. It plays a considerable part in the story of Hereward, the Saxon patriot. Situated on the

[1] "On the Abbey Church of Peterborough." By G. A. Poole, M.A., Arch. Soc. Archdeac. Northampton, 1855, p. 190.

direct line between Bourne, his paternal inheritance, and the Camp of Refuge near Ely, it was exposed to the attacks of both the contending parties. Brando (1066–1069) had made Hereward, who was his nephew, a knight; and the patriot might be credited with a regard for the holy place where he had been girt at a solemn service with the sword and belt of knighthood; but upon Brando's death the abbacy had been granted to a Norman, doubtless with the intention of making the place available as a military centre. Hereward joined the Danes, who had again begun to infest the district, in an attack upon the abbey. The accounts vary as to the time at which this attack was made. One says that it was before Turold, the Norman Abbot, had entered upon possession: another says that Turold had in person joined Ivo Taillebois in an attempt to surprise Hereward and his men in the woods near Bourne, but had been taken prisoner and only released after paying a large ransom. When dismissed there seems to have been something in the nature of an undertaking that the Abbot would not again fight against Hereward; but as soon as he was free he organised fresh attacks, obliging all the tenants of the abbey to supply assistance. In revenge for this Hereward went with his men to Burgh, and laid waste the whole town with fire, plundered all the treasure of the church, and destroyed all the buildings of the abbey except the church itself.

Though Hereward spared the church and went away, yet very soon afterwards the monks, possibly sympathising more with Hereward than with their Norman Abbot (who had left them for a time), allowed themselves to indulge in a drunken revel; and while carousing, a fire seized upon the church and other remaining buildings, from which Gunton says they rescued only a few relics, and little else. But, as Mr Poole has well observed,[1] "we must receive such accounts with some allowance; and, in fact, neither was the abbey so despoiled, nor the church so destroyed, but that there was wealth enough to tempt robbers in the next abbacy, and fuel enough for another conflagration." The robbers in question were foreigners who got into the church by a ladder over the altar of SS. Philip and James, one of them standing with a drawn sword over the sleeping sacrist. The plunder they carried off was valuable, but it was recovered when the thieves were overtaken. The

[1] Poole, p. 193.

King, though he may have punished the robbers, retained the goods so that they were never restored to the abbey.

That Ernulf (1107–1114) should not have done anything towards improving the church is a fact that speaks as plainly as possible of its being already in good condition. Had there been anything like the desolation that some accounts pretend, Ernulf would have spared no exertions in his endeavours to put things right. He came from Canterbury, where he was Prior, and where he had already distinguished himself as a zealous builder; but all that is recorded as due to him at Burgh is the completion of some unfinished buildings, the dormitory, the refectory, and the chapter-house. We may feel confident therefore that the Saxon Church built by Ethelwold remained substantially as first erected until the time of Ernulf's successor; and that the remains to be seen to this day were in their present position when Edgar and Dunstan visited the place.

These newly erected buildings were all that escaped a terrible conflagration that occurred in the time of John of Sais (1114–1125). Hugo Candidus, the chronicler, was an eye-witness of this fire, and has left us an account of it. On the second day of the nones of August, being the vigil of Saint Oswald, King and Martyr (4th Aug. 1116), through neglect, the whole monastery was burnt down, except the chapter-house, dormitory, refectory, and a few outside offices. The refectory had only been in use for three days, having been apparently opened (as we should say in these days) by an entertainment given to the poor. The whole town shared the fate of the monastery. The Abbot was a very passionate man, and being in a great rage, when he was disturbed at a meal by some of the brethren who had come into the refectory to clear the tables, cursed the house, incautiously commended it to the enemy of mankind, and went off immediately to attend to some law-business at Castor. Then one of the servants, who had tried unsuccessfully to light a fire, lost his temper, and (following the evil example of his superior) cried out, "*Veni, Diabole, et insuffla ignem.*" Forthwith the flames rose, and reached to the roof, and spread through all the offices to the town. The whole church was consumed, and the town as well, all the statues (or perhaps *signa* may mean the bells) were broken, and the fire continued burning in the tower for nine days. On the ninth night a mighty wind arose and scattered the fire and burning fragments (*carbones vivos*) from the tower over the Abbot's house, so that there was a fear that nothing would escape the devouring element.

The very next year John of Sais commenced the building of a new minster. He laid the foundation on the 8th of March 1118. Much work was probably necessary before a foundation stone could be laid ; and Abbot John's Chronicle, wherein it is said that the foundation of the new church at Burgh was laid, on the 12th of March, 1117, may be speaking of the actual commencement of the operations ; and Candidus, who gives the later date, and who was present, may refer to a ceremonial laying of a stone, after the ground had been cleared and new designs prepared. The church then begun is the minster we now see. The works commenced, as we find almost universally the case, at the east end. The choir is here terminated by an apse ; and before the eastern addition was built in the fifteenth century, this apse, with the two lesser ones at the ends of the choir aisles, must have presented an appearance of much grandeur.

The Abbot who began the church did not live to see much progress made, as he died in 1125. He is said to have worked hard at it, but how much was finished we do not know. The next Abbot, after an interval of two years, was Henry of Anjou, a kinsman of King Henry I. He appears to have been a scandalous pluralist, restless and greedy, continually seeking and obtaining additional preferment, and as often being forced to resign. He was not the man to prosecute such a work as was to be done at Burgh ; " he lived even as a drone in a hive ; as the drone eateth and draggeth forward to himself all that is brought near, even so did he."[1] It is likely that for eight years after the death of John de Sais nothing was done to advance the building. But the Prior of S. Neots, Martin de Bec, who was appointed to succeed Henry, was continually employed in building about the monastery ; and in particular he completed the presbytery of the church, and brought back the sacred relics, and the monks, on Saint Peter's day into the new church, with great joy. Alexander, Bishop of Lincoln, was present ; but there was no service of consecration. According to the Saxon Chronicle this took place in 1140 ; Abbot John says in 1143.

[1] Anglo-Saxon Chronicle, anno 1128.

Before proceeding further with the architectural history of the cathedral (as distinguished from the description of it, which will be given in due course), it may be well to say a few words upon the principles which have guided the writer in his treatment of the subject. These cannot be better expressed than in a very pithy sentence uttered by Professor Willis at the meeting of the Archæological Institute at this very place in 1861. " In all investigations of this nature, I am of opinion that it is requisite to ascertain first whether there exist any contemporary documents which may throw light upon the history of the fabric, and then to let the stones tell their own tale." Now there is an abundance of documentary evidence for our purpose; but recent criticism has shewn that not all is to be relied upon as authentic. And the Latin expressions for different portions of the building can, in many instances, not be interpreted with certainty; while the absence of all reference to some works of importance (the West Front, for example), is very mysterious. Most of these documents had been studied in manuscript by Gunton and Patrick, and the result of their studies was published in 1686. The work is entitled "The History of the church of Peterburgh . . . By Symon Gunton, late Prebendary of that church . . . . And set forth by Symon Patrick, D.D. now Dean of the same." Gunton was Prebendary from 1646 to his death in 1676; Patrick was Dean from 1679 till his consecration as Bishop of Chichester in 1689. Most of the documents in question have since been printed. Two writers in the last half century have published monographs on the cathedral, both of great value, both treating the subject after Professor Willis's method. These are G. A. Poole, formerly Vicar of Welford, whose paper on the Abbey Church of Peterborough was published among the Transactions of the Architectural Society of the Archdeaconry of Northampton in 1855, and the late Professor F. A. Paley, a second edition of whose pamphlet, "Remarks on the Architecture of Peterborough Cathedral," was issued in 1859. It by no means detracts from the value of the method employed that the results of the investigations of these two careful students of the fabric do not accord with one another. Much must always be left to inference or conjecture. Since they wrote many discoveries have been made which have shewn some of their conclusions to have been inaccurate. But the rule is a sound one, and indeed it is only by studying the documents and the fabric together that one can hope to learn the history of any great building.

Thus, when the chronicle records that Abbot Martin completed the presbytery, and that then the monks entered into the new church, we should naturally understand that he built no more than the existing choir and its aisles. But there can be little doubt that his work included the eastern bays and aisles of both transepts. The style of the architecture speaks for itself, "the stones tell their own tale," and the most careful study, and the most painstaking investigations, have failed to detect the slightest break in the continuity or character of the work. This applies to the whole of the eastern part of the transepts, excepting of course the alterations that were made in later times. As Martin remained abbot till 1155, it is probable that he went on with his building after the choir had been opened, and that this work in the transepts was done in the latter part of his abbacy, but there is no record of it.

Of Abbot William of Waterville (1155–1175) we are told that in his time were erected the transepts (*ambæ cruces*) and three stages of the central tower (*tres ystoriæ magistræ turris*). This does not contradict what has been said above as to the eastern part of the transepts being built in Abbot Martin's time. For the walls and aisles to the east only would be in position; and his successor might well be credited with the erection of the transepts, if he built the ends and western walls, and roofed in the whole. It is tolerably clear also that this same abbot must have built the two bays of the nave adjoining the central tower. A tower of three stages, presumably of the massive character that marks all large Norman towers, must have had some western supports. Two bays of the nave would act as buttresses; and it is easy to see the difference between these two bays and the rest of the nave. Apart from many minute points of difference which only an expert architectural student could fully appreciate, there is one conspicuous variation which all can see. This is in the tympanum of the triforium arches; in all four instances we notice rugged ornamentation here which occurs nowhere else in the nave.

Exclusive of the western transept we may assign eighty years as the period during which the Norman Minster was being erected. And it is one of the most noteworthy points in connection with its architectural history, and one that has produced the happiest result in the grandeur of the whole effect of the building upon the spectator, that each successive architect carried on faithfully the ideas of his predecessors. The whole work has been continued, as it were, in the spirit of one design; and the differences in details, while quite observable when once pointed out, are yet so unobtrusive that they seldom attract notice. To mention one such instance, Mr Paley calls attention to the different ornamentation on the windows of the south transept when compared with those in the north transept, as well as to the fact that on the south those windows have straight sides to the inner surface of the wall, while those on the north have the sides splayed. He justly argues, from these and other considerations, that the south transept was built first.

To Abbot William of Waterville succeeded Benedict (1177–1193). Of him we are told that he built the whole nave in stone and wood-work, from the tower of the choir to the front, and also erected a rood-loft. He built also the great gate-way at the west of the precincts, with the chapel of S. Nicolas above it, the chapel of S. Thomas of Canterbury and the hospital attached to it, the great hall with the buildings connected; and he also commenced that wonderful work (*illud mirificum opus*) near the brewery, but his death occurred before it could be completed. What this last named great work was we do not know. It is at least possible that the reference is to the western transept.

Considerable controversy has arisen as to the work in the church thus attributed to Benedict. Both chronicles give him credit for building the whole nave from the tower of the choir to the front. The wording, however, of the two is so similar as to cause some doubt as to their being independent authorities. Granting that some small portion of the nave to the east, as before described, must have been built as a support to Waterville's tower, the question remains, what is the front to which this record alludes? There is of course no doubt that the words speak of the nave only, exclusive of the front. But was this the present west front, as now remaining, or was there previously a Norman front to the church? There is much to be said on both sides. Mr Paley believes the latter; Mr Poole, the former. And possibly the true solution may be found in a combination of both theories, though at first sight that seems impossible. That a west front in Norman times was designed, and in part built, Mr Paley has shewn most conclusively. He indeed thinks it was finished, but that is open to considerable doubt. The evidence on which he proves that two western towers were at least designed is quite conclusive; and the whole passage in which he discusses the matter may be quoted.[1] " Proceeding towards the west end of the nave, we observe a very singular feature. The third pillar from the west end on each side is considerably larger and wider than the others; and it also projects further into the aisles. The arch also, springing from it westward, is of a much greater span. The opposite vaulting shafts, in the aisle walls, are brought forward, beyond the line of the rest, to meet the pillars in question; so that the arch across the aisles is, in this part, very much contracted, and, instead of being a mere groin rib, like the rest, is a strong moulded arch of considerable depth in the soffit. What appears at first sight, still more strange, the wall of the aisles opposite to the wider nave-arch just mentioned, is brought forward at least a foot internally, but again retires to the old level at the last bay; so that in this particular part the whole thickness of the aisle-wall is considerably greater. Not less remarkable is the circumstance, that the half-pillars on each side of this wider arch resume the complex[2] form already described at the eastern end of the nave, though they do not accurately agree either in plan or details. . . . Now it seems highly probable that it was at this very spot that it [*i.e.*, a Norman west front] stood, with two flanking Norman towers at the end of the aisles. The wider nave-arch, with its massive and complex pillars, was the entrance into the tower from each side of the nave. The thicker aisle-wall opposite to it was, in fact, *the tower wall*. The larger and heavier group of vaulting-shafts against the aisle-wall, and the strong arch spanning the aisle across this point in place of the groin-rib, were all parts of the tower. . . . The transformation of the base of these two immense towers into a compartment of the aisle, so similar to all the rest that its real nature

---

[1] "Remarks on the Architecture of Peterborough Cathedral." By F. A. Paley, M.A. 2nd Ed., 1859, p. 21.
[2] The two eastern pillars of the nave are circular; and the third pillar from the tower, on both sides, is "composed of nook-shafts set in rectangular recesses against the body of the pier."

has never been hitherto suspected, is highly ingenious. It is only when once detected that the anomalies above mentioned are at all intelligible."

These arguments prove to demonstration that the intention was to make the Norman church end at the spot where now stand the third pillars of the nave ; and that the two western towers had begun to be built. As an after thought another bay was added to the nave, with western transept, and last of all the grand west front was another after thought. But they do not establish the fact that the towers were ever finished, or the Norman west front actually erected. The considerations adduced are perfectly consistent with the theory that the additional length of the nave was decided upon while the towers were still unfinished, and the lower part of the towers transformed as Mr Paley has described. Thus we combine the rival theories. For Mr Poole[1] maintains that the point, up to which Benedict's work was carried, must mean the front we now see. One argument he advances appears unanswerable.[2] Of the two chroniclers, Swapham takes his history down to 1246; Abbot John ruled from 1249 to 1262. Both these writers therefore, beyond all question, were alive when the present front was finished. "Here are two people writing after the present west front was erected, and for persons before whose eyes the present west front appeared every day, and speaking of the tower and of the west front as well-known limits to a certain work. Surely they not only meant, but *must have meant*, the front that *then* was, in other words, the west front as it is *now*."

The conclusion of the controversy may perhaps not yet have been reached. But all the difficulties appear to be explained by understanding that Benedict's work extended to the west end of the present nave, and that he carried the whole building further west than was originally intended, and managed to do this without destroying the lower part of the towers which had actually been raised.

[1] Some of Mr Poole's reasoning, as to the different parts of the nave to be attributed to different abbots, depends upon an assumption that the Saxon church was on the site of the present one, and that some part of the nave was still existing in a ruinous condition while the present choir and tower were being built. Recent discoveries have proved that this assumption is groundless, for the nave of the Saxon church was beyond the south aisle of the existing nave.

[2] Poole, p. 204.

When, therefore, the Norman nave, as originally designed, was approaching completion, the designers determined upon an extension of the nave, and a much grander western finish to the church than had before been contemplated. This idea included a dignified western transept, the dimensions of which, from north to south, should exceed the entire width of the nave and aisles. This would of necessity involve the lengthening of the nave, because the monastic buildings came close to the south aisle of the nave, at the point where the original termination of the church was to have been, as may be seen by the old western wall of the cloister, which is still standing.

The two next abbots were Andrew (1193–1200), and Acharius (1200–1210). To one or both of these may be assigned the western transept. By their time the Norman style was giving place to the lighter and more elegant architecture of the Early English period, the round arch was beginning to be superseded by the pointed arch, and the massive ornamentation which marks the earlier style was displaced by the conventional foliage that soon came to be very generally employed. Most wisely, however, the Peterborough builders made their work at the west end of the nave intentionally uniform with what was already built. Very numerous indications of this can be seen by careful observers. The bases of the western pillars, the change in the depth of the mouldings, characteristic changes in the capitals in the triforium range, and especially the grand arches below the transept towers, which are pointed, but enriched with ornamentation of pronounced Norman character, all point to the later date of this western transept.

At the west wall of the church all trace of Norman work disappears. The arcade near the ground, the large round arch above the door, the great west window and its adjacent arches (not, of course, including the late tracery), are all of distinct Early English character. The whole of this wall may be held to be an integral part of the west front, and not of the transept which it bounds.

When we come to the most distinctive feature of the cathedral, the glorious west front, we find we have no help whatever from the chronicles. Nowhere is there the smallest reference to its building. Other works raised by the Abbots of the period are named, but the noble western portico is never once mentioned. Perhaps the rapid succession of abbots after

Acharius may account for this. The building must have taken some years, and the credit of the whole cannot be given to one. There were four Abbots after Acharius before the church was dedicated. They were Robert of Lindsey (1214–1222), Alexander (1222–1226), Martin of Ramsey (1226–1233), and Walter of S. Edmunds (1233–1245). During the abbacy of this last the church was dedicated on the 4th of October 1237, (according to the *Chronicon Angliæ Petriburgense*), or on the 28th of Septemper 1238, according to Matthew Paris. The Bishop of Lincoln, Robert Grostête, took the chief part in the ceremony, assisted by William Brewer, Bishop of Exeter. The other chronicle calls the second bishop suffragan of the Bishop of Lincoln, which may mean no more than that he assisted on the occasion. The dedication took place in accordance with the provisions of certain constitutions which had been drawn up at a council held in London. No doubt the building had before this been completed. This date agrees well with the period which all architectural experts accept as the probable date of the erection of the west front. It may have been, and probably was, finished some few years before the dedication. The very fine gables at the north and south ends of the western transept are of the same date as the west front.

Considerable changes in the fabric, as well as additional buildings, belong to the latter part of the thirteenth century. The documents mention two of these. In the time of Richard of London (1274–1295), but before his election to the abbacy, while he was still sacrist, the bell-tower was erected, in which were hung the great bells which were called Les Londreis, because he was himself a Londoner, and had caused them to be brought from London. A previous abbot, John of Calais (1249–1262), had contributed a great bell to the monastery, which he had dedicated to S. Oswald. On it was inscribed the rhyming hexameter *Jon de Caux abbas Oswaldo consecrat hoc vas*. The other great work of this period was a magnificent Lady Chapel, since destroyed, begun in 1272 by William Parys, then Prior, who laid the first stone with his own hand, and placed beneath it some writings from the gospels. He lived to see it completed, and at last his body was interred within it. Its altar was consecrated in 1290, as is recorded in the register of Bishop Oliver Sutton. It is described as having been built of stone and wood, with a leaden roof, and with glass windows. There was a statue of the Virgin, and round the walls, or perhaps in the stained glass in the windows, there were figures of those named in the genealogy, with a compendium of their lives beneath each. The Prior contributed five pounds of silver and upwards of his annual revenues towards the decoration of this chapel. From an engraving in Gunton's History, which may be taken as fairly representing its appearance, for it was standing in his time, although the drawing is manifestly inaccurate and must have been sketched from memory, we gather that the windows were of the same character as four which are still to be seen, three of them in the eastern chapels of the south transept, and the fourth on the north side, near the site of the Lady Chapel. These are all of excellent geometric work, and precisely of the date given. This chapel was built, as at Ely, to the east of the north transept. The position of the roof can be traced on the east wall of the transept; and it can be there seen how the Norman clerestory windows were originally arranged. These being covered by the Lady Chapel, had not been altered like those in other parts of the church.

Other works of this century, not mentioned in the annals, are the entire removal of the lower stage of Norman windows in the aisles, these were replaced by wide windows of five lights each; the addition of a parapet to the apse; the erection of piscinas and other accompaniments to side altars, at the east ends of the choir aisles.

For the rest of the architectural history we have no chronicles to guide us, and are left to the stones themselves. But there is very little difficulty in fixing at least approximate dates for all the later work. The most important alteration in the fourteenth century was the removal of the stages above the four great arches of the central tower, and the substitution of a lighter lantern. When this was done, the great round arches east and west of the tower were changed into pointed arches, but those north and south were left unaltered. There is every probability that some signs of insecurity had made themselves evident. We have seen that three stages of the Norman tower were erected by Abbot William of Waterville. Though not so stated we infer from this that at least one more stage was afterwards added. In any case the tower must have been a very massive structure, considerably higher than the present one. In the early part of this century, in 1321, the great tower of Ely had fallen; and its fate may have warned the monks of Peterborough to see that the disaster was not repeated here. This alteration must have been made, judging by the details of the architecture, in the second quarter of the century. Above the lantern was a wooden octagon. The views that are given of this hardly warrant the admiration that has been sometimes expressed, or the regrets that have been uttered at its removal. It may have been designed to carry a wooden spire, such as was afterwards erected on the bell-tower. But most will agree with the criticism that it was "a low and unsightly structure." It hardly rose more than eight or ten feet above the top of the lantern, and the whole height of the central tower, including the octagon, was less than the height of the south-western spire of the front.

To this century belongs the transformation of the triforium windows all through the nave and choir. Parapets were at the same time added above the Norman corbel tables. The change effected in the apse was the most noticeable; not only were the two upper tiers of Norman windows replaced by Decorated ones of larger size, but the three lowest ones in the centre were altogether removed, and their place taken by lofty archways, when the new building was built. But we can judge of their appearance from the two side windows which still remain; these, being not now external, have had all the glass removed; but the mullions and tracery are perfect, and even the iron-bars across are still there. At the inner surface of the wall the five lower windows have very good hanging tracery, of different designs.

The south-western spire of the west front is also of this period, probably a little earlier in date than the lantern. This is of very remarkable beauty, and very much more elegant than the corresponding spire to the north. The triangular section of the pinnacles at the base of the spire, the crockets with which they are enriched, and the open canopies around, combine to produce a most graceful feature. To the latter years of this century may be assigned the central porch, with room above, inserted between the two middle piers of the west front. Some regard this as a blemish; others as a distinct improvement. One party maintains[1] that it is "an unsightly encumbrance, in its present position, seeing that it violates the uniformity of design displayed in the west front"; the other party contends[2] that it is "an extremely judicious insertion, and that it really does, just as if it was intended for that purpose only, restore its proper dignity to the central arch of the façade." It was most likely built as a matter of structural necessity, to

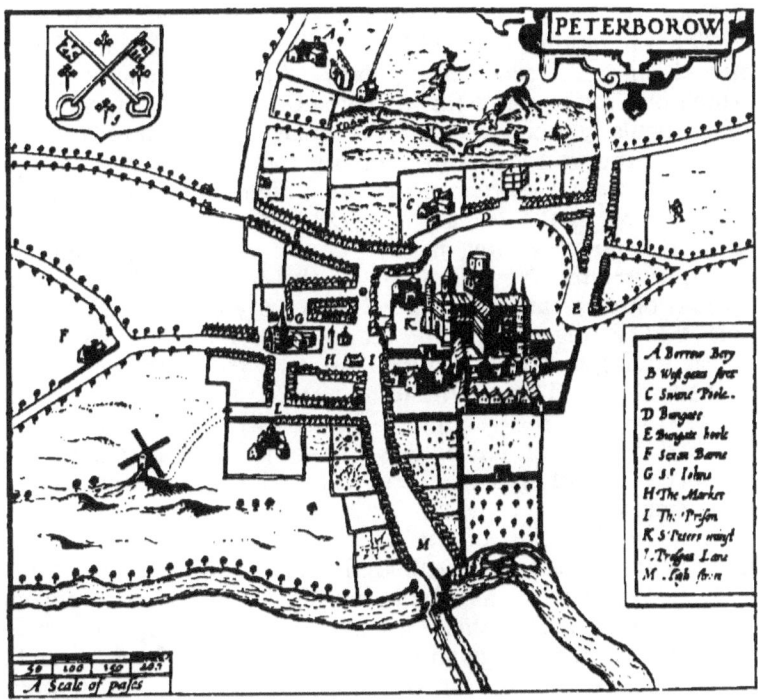

FROM SPEED'S MAP, 1610.

secure the stability of the front. From a settlement of the foundations, or from a failure of the two central piers, or from the great weight of masonry above, for there are no western buttresses, the whole must have been in danger of falling. Mr Paley points out that the "construction of this elegant little edifice is extremely scientific, especially in the manner in which

[1] Paley, p. 54. [2] Poole, p. 216.

the thrust is distributed through the medium of the side turrets so as to fall upon the buttresses in front. These turrets being erected against one side of the triangular columns, on the right and the left hand, support them in two directions at once, viz., from collapsing towards each other, and from falling forward. The latter pressure is thrown wholly upon the buttresses in front, which project seven feet beyond the base of the great pillars." The room above is called by Browne Willis the Consistory Court. It is now used for the Minster Library.

The alterations and additions during the Perpendicular period can be detected at a glance. All the Norman windows which had remained unaltered were now filled with tracery, not of particularly good design; the great west window and the others in the west wall were similarly treated; the conical tops to the transeptal corner turrets were altered into battlements; the screens in the transepts were made, and, probably, the groined wooden ceiling in the choir. The most important addition was the New Building at the east end of the choir. This is often erroneously called the Lady Chapel; but when this edifice was erected the Lady Chapel to the east of the north transept, and for more than 150 years afterwards, was still standing. The new building was begun by Abbot Ashton (1438–1471), whose rebus is to be seen in its decorations, and finished by Abbot Kirton (1496–1528). In the seventeenth century the windows were filled with stained glass, but none of this remains.

In 1541, the reign of the abbots came to an end, and the abbey church became a cathedral. For a hundred years the church itself, as well as all the buildings attached to it, appear to have remained in their full glory. There is no reason to discredit the account given of the preservation of this church, when so many others were dismantled or sold at the suppression of the monasteries. It was suggested to King Henry VIII., after the interment here of Queen Katherine of Arragon, that it would become his greatness to erect a suitable monument of her in the place where she was buried; and in reply the King said he would leave her one of the goodliest monuments in Christendom, meaning that he would spare the church for her sake. We conclude, however, from what we know of the state of the fabric in the reign of Charles I., that although no buildings may have been demolished, yet the church itself

THE WEST PROSPECT, OR FRONT, OF THE CATHEDRAL CHURCH OF
PETERBOROUGH IN THE SEVENTEENTH CENTURY.

was falling into disrepair. No doubt the diminished resources of the establishment, as well as the numerous demands upon the stipends (never large) of the members of the chapter, most of whom had duties and claims elsewhere besides having families to support, materially reduced the amount that could be annually devoted to the sustentation of the fabric. In the time of the civil war much wanton destruction took place. Nearly everything in the nature of ornamentation or embellishment was destroyed. A full account of the mischief wrought has been preserved. Without particularly naming such things as books, documents, vestments, and the movable ornaments, we find the damage done to the fabric itself was terrible indeed. The organs, "of which there were two pair," were broken down. All the stalls of the choir, the altar rails, and the great brass chandelier, were knocked to pieces. The altar of course did not escape. Of the reredos, or altar-piece, and its destruction, Patrick writes as follows: "Now behind the Communion Table, there stood a curious piece of stone-work, admired much by strangers and travellers; a stately skreen it was, well wrought, painted and gilt, which rose up as high almost as the roof of the church in a row of three lofty spires, with other lesser spires, growing out of each of them, as it is represented in the annexed draught.[1] This had now no Imagery-work upon it, or anything else that might justly give offence, and yet because it bore the name of the High Altar, was pulled all down with ropes, lay'd low and level with the ground." All the tombs were mutilated or hacked down. The hearse over the tomb of Queen Katherine was demolished, as well as the arms and escutcheons which still remained above the spot where Mary Queen of Scots had been buried. All the other chief monuments were defaced in like manner. One in particular is worth mentioning. It was a monument in the new building erected to himself by Sir Humfrey Orme in his lifetime. Two words on the inscription, "Altar" and "Sacrifice," are said to have excited the fury of the rabble, and it was broken down with axes, pole-axes, and hammers. So this good old knight "outlived his own monument, and lived to

---

[1] The engraving that accompanies this description represents a dignified altar-piece, but seems taken from a rough drawing, or possibly from memory. On the altar were two tapers burning, an alms dish, and two books. The Abbot's chair, of stone, is to the south, facing west.

see himself carried in effigie on a Souldiers back, to the publick market-place, there to be sported withall, a Crew of Souldiers going before in procession, some with surplices, some with organ pipes, to make up the solemnity." This monument, as it was left after this profanity, is still to be seen exactly as it remained when the soldiers had done their work. The brasses in the floor, the bells in the steeple, were regarded as

IRON RAILINGS.   DRAWN BY O. R. ALLBROW.

lawful plunder. The same would not be said of the stained glass, of which there was a great quantity. This was especially the case with the windows in the cloisters, which were "most famed of all, for their great art and pleasing variety." All the glass was broken to pieces. Much that escaped the violence of these irresponsible zealots fell before the more regular proceedings of commissioners. By their orders many of the buildings belonging to the cathedral were pulled down and the materials sold. This was the case with the cloisters, the chapter-house, the Bishop's hall and chapel. The merchant that bought the lead from the palace roofs did not make a very prosperous bargain, for he lost it all (as Dean Patrick says, within his own knowledge) and the ship which carried it, on the voyage to Holland.

For some time nothing was done to repair the damage. At length the Chief Justice of the Common Pleas, Oliver St. John, obtained a grant of the ruined Minster, which he gave to the town for use as a parish church, their own parish church having also gone to decay. This gentleman was doubly allied to the Cromwell family, his first wife being great-grand-daughter of Sir Henry Cromwell, of Hinchinbrooke, and his second wife daughter of Henry Cromwell, of Upwood. He had been sent upon a distasteful embassy to Holland, where he experienced many indignities; and on his return, according to Mark Noble,[1] "he protested, that all the favour which he received in reward for this embassy, was, that he obtained the cathedral of Peterborough, which was propounded to be sold and demolished, to be granted to the citizens of that place." The interest that he took in Peterborough arose from the fact that he resided at Longthorpe Hall, about two miles off.

The burden of restoring the church to a decent condition being too great for the inhabitants, they agreed to pull down the Lady Chapel, and sell the materials. This was done, except that some portion of the woodwork was utilised in repairs. The painted boards from the roof were made into backs for the seats in the choir. An engraving of the choir as it appeared in the eighteenth century shews these boards. They are mostly adorned with the letter M surmounted by a crown, and the three lions of England, in alternate lozenges. Until the Restoration the church was served by a schoolmaster of the Charterhouse, Samuel Wilson, appointed by the London Committee. When the cathedral body was restored, further repairs were gradually effected, and when Dean Patrick wrote, he says that the church was "recovering her ancient beauty and lustre again."

But the same causes which operated to prevent very much being done for years after the dissolution of monasteries, the

[1] "Memoirs of the Protectoral-House of Cromwell," ii. 18.

absence of any special fabric fund, and the inadequacy of the revenues, again produced the same results. Browne Willis published his survey of this cathedral in 1742. He says that considering the pillaging of the church by King Henry VIII., and the subsequent despoiling by King Edward VI., and Queen Elizabeth, "we may less wonder that so large a fabrick has not had more care taken of it as it ought; for I cannot but say, that it is ill kept in repair, and lies very slovenly in the inside, and several of the windows are stopped up with bricks, and the glazing in others sadly broken; and the boards in the roof of the middle Isle or Nave, which with the Cross Isle is not archt with stone (but wainscotted with painted boards, as at S. Albans) are several of them damaged and broken, as is also the pavement; insomuch that scarce any cathedral in England is more neglected." He proceeds to say that the Dean and Chapter had recently set apart £700 for repairs, and intended to apply more money to the same purpose when certain leases were expired.

While Willis was collecting information for his book, Francis Lockier was Dean. In his time new seats were erected in the choir which were "very plain and tasteless." They remained until 1827. A new organ was also obtained. £1500 was spent on these alterations.

The record of other changes, until the time of Dean Monk, is meagre. Dean Tarrant (1764-1791) collected the fragments of stained glass and had them all inserted in the windows of the apse. He also repaved the church, but most unfortunately without carefully preserving the ancient inscribed monumental stones. An altar screen and organ screen, from designs by Carter, were erected; but neither seems to have possessed much merit.

Dean Kipling (1798-1822) is chiefly remembered from his alterations to the lantern tower. He erected unsightly turrets at the four corners and removed the octagon. These turrets, commonly spoken of with derision as "Dean Kipling's chimneys" were of unsuitable height, and poor detail; they were terminated with battlements. They were happily removed when the tower was rebuilt.

Dean Monk (1822-1830) inaugurated and carried out an extensive scheme of reparation. The appeal to the public for subscriptions is dated 31st July 1827. It states that the altar screen, choir screen, and all the woodwork in the choir are unworthy of the structure to which they belong: that the Dean and Chapter had substantially repaired the exterior of the church at their own expense; that they had procured plans from Mr Blore, and an estimate of upwards of £5000 for the projected work. The members of the chapter in their corporate capacity had given £1000, and had further individually subscribed £1050. The result of this appeal was that by June 1828 a sum of £5021 11s. had been collected.

The improvements effected before this appeal to the public was made are enumerated by Britton. As has been intimated, the cost was defrayed by Dean Monk and the Chapter from their own resources. The chief repairs and restorations were these:—new roofs were put to the transepts and bell-tower; columns, mouldings, and ornaments in various parts of the church were renewed; several windows, till then blocked up with rubble, were opened and glazed, and in some cases the stonework made good; the pinnacles, spires, and shafts of the west front were carefully restored; two Norman doorways, which had been obscured for ages, were exposed to view. The work in the choir included new stalls and seats, pulpit, and throne; an altar screen of clunch, filling up the lower part of the apse; and an organ screen, also of clunch, with an open parapet, and enriched with much diaper-work and many canopies, and adorned on the west face with large shields of arms,[1] very brightly coloured, charged with the heraldic bearings of the principal subscribers. At first there were only four stalls on each side of the entrance to the choir; others were added, in front of the ladies' pews, when Honorary Canons were created in 1844. This organ-loft did not occupy the place of the former screen, which was where the monastic choir had always terminated, at the second bay west of the tower, but was placed under the eastern arch of the lantern tower. The former screen was called by Rickman "a barbarous piece of painted wood-work." It was either sold, or taken by the contractors as a perquisite; it ultimately found its way into a little garden at Woodston, just across the river, where it was transformed into a summer-house, or arbour.[2]

Great admiration was universally expressed at the conclusion

---

[1] These shields, which were of metal, are now arranged on the walls of the library.

[2] Where the author has often seen it. It was at last destroyed in a fire.

of this work. It was esteemed a marvel of beauty. Harriet Martineau, in her "History of England during the Thirty Years' Peace," thought the re-opening of the choir a matter of sufficient national importance to be recorded in her book. She writes thus: "A new choir of great beauty, was erected in Peterborough Cathedral during this period, and the church was made once more what it was before it was devastated by the Puritans." All must admire the enthusiasm and devotion which brought this restoration to a successful issue, although to the taste of the present day it would all appear cumbrous and heavy.

In the time of Dean Saunders (1853-1878) the choir roof was painted anew, and much valuable and important work was done towards securing the stability of the fabric, by underpinning some of the walls, and in other ways; but all the expense was defrayed out of the resources of the Dean and Chapter, and no public appeal was made for assistance. Indications of the insecurity of the lantern-tower had begun to appear, one or more fragments of the masonry having fallen from a great height; and for some years before the tower was condemned as unsafe, a wooden stage had been erected, above the four great arches, as a protection in case more stones should fall. The great pier to the south-east had been, time out of memory, bound all round with strong iron bands. As far back as 1593, there is an entry among the cathedral accounts, which mentions that £47 4s. 9d. had been spent on "the great column near the choir repaired with iron and timber." In 1882 the evidences of failure in the lantern stage were found to be increasing, and its condition was pronounced dangerous. Large gaps made their appearance towards the end of the year, and in January 1883, the greater part of the tower was said to be in a "state of movement."

It was very soon realised that nothing short of rebuilding the tower from the foundation would meet the case. The first stone was taken down on April 5th, and the tower and two eastern piers were removed by August. The western piers were soon afterwards condemned, and taken down the following year. The chief corner stone of the new tower at the northeastern pier, was laid with full masonic ceremonial on May 7th 1884, by the Earl of Carnarvon, acting for the Prince of Wales. All the stones, as taken down, were numbered, and every one that could be used again was replaced in its original position.

During this year there commenced a controversy as to the correct way of finishing the building of the tower. When the Decorated lantern was first built, the great arches, east and west, to the choir and nave, were altered from the round to the pointed shape. A few of the stones of the original Norman arches having been brought to light during the work, some persons wished round arches to be built as at first. Some stones of the Norman tower were also found; and it was proposed to heighten the central tower by one stage of work in the Norman style, using original stones where possible, and placing the Decorated stage above it. Others again, wanted a lofty central spire to be added. The matter was referred to Archbishop Benson for his decision. In the result the whole was rebuilt exactly as before, with the exception that the four corner turrets, erected by Dean Kipling, were not replaced.

In 1886 the tower was finished. The transept ceilings were repaired in this and the next year. All unsound wood was removed and replaced by good oak. The diamond shapes are still to be seen, but the black, white, and brown patterns have been improved away. The discovery of the site of the Saxon church, which will be described hereafter, was made in 1887. Steady progress continued to be made in securing the safety of various parts of the church; and on July 11th, 1889, a temporary choir having been fitted up, divine service was again held in the ancient ritual choir, which extended two bays into the nave.

During the next two years many contributors to the general fund for the restoration, and some others, made gifts of special objects for the embellishment of the choir. By the end of May, 1892, the mosaic pavement was almost completed, and the bishop's throne, the pulpit, the litany desk, and eighteen stalls had been erected. These gifts were solemnly dedicated at a stately service held on June 2nd, when, after the litany and an anthem, the special service was taken by the Archbishop of Canterbury at the altar, and after that *Te Deum* was sung. A sermon was preached by the Bishop of Durham, formerly Canon. The Archbishop and Bishops wore their convocation robes.

Two years later the fitting up of the choir was very nearly complete, four stalls only remaining to be supplied. At a second dedication of gifts on May 10th, 1894, these additional gifts were in position; new organ and case, canopied reredos, retable, iron screens inclosing the four eastern bays of the choir,

pillars and choir gates (part of a design for an elaborate screen), eight stalls, extension of mosaic pavement, fourteen sub-stalls and seats for lay-clerks and choristers, altar-rails, and credence table. Up to this date, since the commencement of the restoration in 1883, upwards of £32,400 had been expended upon the fabric, besides more than £17,800 upon the internal fittings of the choir. All the woodwork of the choir is now quite complete.

In speaking of the work that is now being done at the west front we touch upon a very delicate matter, and one that has given rise to no little controversy. The state of insecurity had been known for years. In the early part of 1896, a scaffold was raised in order to enable Mr Pearson, the architect of the cathedral, to make a complete examination of the front, special causes for alarm having lately been detected. At first it was believed that underpinning the central piers would secure the stability of the whole. This was done, as well as the shoring and strutting to the gables of the two outer arches. The clearing away of the dirt and rubbish, and the cleaning of the groining, disclosed greater danger than had been expected, and the architect recommended the rebuilding of parts of the gables. Before acting on this advice the Restoration Committee took the opinion of Sir A. W. Blomfield, and his report not only confirmed the opinion expressed by Mr Pearson, but said further that much of the superstructure was so disintegrated, that it was impossible to render substantial and lasting repair as it stood, "and that the inner parts of the walls were such as would not permit of the superstructure being preserved or successfully dealt with by any of the well-known expedients frequently recommended and sometimes employed with success." When it became generally known that the Dean and Chapter intended to act upon the advice given in these two reports, the knowledge created the greatest possible excitement. Other plans were suggested; the mere removal of a single stone to make it more secure was declared quite unnecessary; the taking down a gable to rebuild it was denounced as Vandalism. Much strong language and many hard words were used which had better be forgotten. It certainly seems difficult to explain how the objectors to the course that had been decided upon could write of the west front that it was "superficially, in a fair state of preservation," or that it was "literally without a patch or blemish." The present writer was for twenty years a member of the cathedral foundation, and lived just opposite the west front. He made a special study of the history and fabric of the cathedral. Hardly a year passed without something falling down; sometimes a piece of a pinnacle, sometimes a crocket or other ornament, sometimes a shaft. Old engravings of the

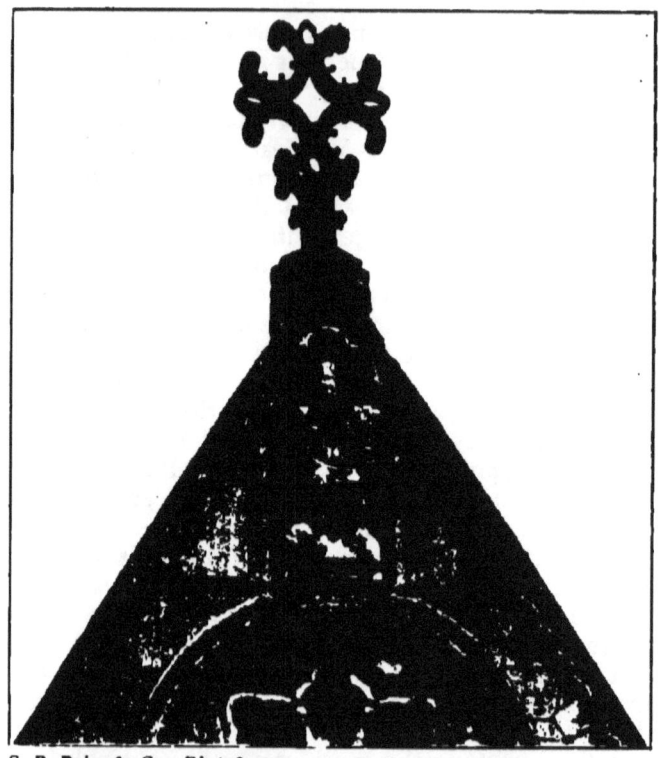

S. B. Bolas & Co., Photo.]
FINIAL OF THE CENTRAL GABLE OF WEST FRONT.

spires show the pinnacles broken. Many of the shafts are wanting. Some have been replaced in wood. Many wholly new ones were put up by Dean Monk. And concerning the north arch, which was notoriously the most dangerous, Dean Patrick has recorded that Bishop Laney gave £100 toward the repairing one of the great arches of the church porch "which was faln down in the late times." Dean Monk also, in a memoir of his predecessor Dean Duport,[1] speaks of the efforts of the cathedral body to repair the devastation caused by the civil war, and says "in particular one of the three large arches of the West Front, the beauty of which is acknowledged to be without rival, having fallen down, it was restored in all its original magnificence." In an account of the cathedral published by the writer thirty years ago, he says of this arch: "Its present state looks dangerous from below. The stones in the arch have some sad gaps. It is tied up by iron bands, and further protected within by a great number of wooden pegs, not of recent construction. When last observed it leant forward $14\frac{1}{2}$ inches." In 1893 he wrote: "there is no doubt that the security of the whole front is a most serious question that before long must demand energetic action."

A very great preponderance of local opinion is in favour of the action of the Dean and Chapter. When it came to moving the stones, after all the rubbish was removed, it was found that the mortar had crumbled into mere dust, and could be swept away; and that the stones themselves could be lifted from their positions, without the use of any tool. What has actually been done is this: the north gable has been taken down, and the outer orders of the moulding of the arch for some feet, and rebuilt; the innermost order has not been moved. Relieving arches have been put in at the back. The gable is now believed to be perfectly secure. The cross on the summit was replaced in its position on July 2nd, 1897. This is what has been called "the destruction" of the west front.

[1] Museum Criticum, viii., 672.

CHAPTER II.

THE CATHEDRAL—EXTERIOR.

NEARLY every cathedral and large abbey church has some one conspicuous feature by which it is remembered, and with which it is specially associated in the minds of most persons. Nearly every one also claims for itself to have the best example of some one architectural feature, or the largest, or the oldest, or in some other way the most remarkable. Occasionally the claim is indisputable, because the boasted object is unique in the country; as is the case with the octagon at Ely, the three spires at Lichfield, the situation and western Galilee of Durham, and the almost perfect unity of design at Salisbury. Sometimes, if not unique, there is no question as to the justice of the claim for superiority; whether it be for a thing of beauty, like the cloisters at Gloucester, or the Norman tower at Norwich, or the east window of Carlisle, or the angel-choir at Lincoln; or for size or extent, when the question narrows itself to a mere matter of measurement.

But it is not always by any means the fact that this prominent feature, though it is the pride of the inhabitants and a source of admiration to visitors, is really the most noteworthy thing belonging to the church. This seems specially the case at Peterborough. Probably nobody speaks or thinks of Peterborough cathedral without immediately associating it with its glorious west front. Many believe that there is little else in the building that is worthy of any particular attention. And yet nowhere in the kingdom is there to be found a finer and more complete Norman church. Arches, windows, mouldings, more elaborate and more grand may no doubt be found elsewhere; but where else can we find, as here, choir, transepts, and nave, with all the original Norman, from ground to roof, with two insignificant exceptions, remaining unaltered? It is natural to compare the three great East Anglian Cathedrals, as all have superb work of the Norman period. But at Norwich the lower arches in the choir have been rebuilt in the Perpendicular style, while the vaulted roof of the nave, raised in the fifteenth century, is less in keeping with the sturdy architecture beneath it than the wooden ceiling at Peterborough. At Ely, beautiful as is the work in the octagon and choir, there is no Norman work east of the transepts. Of course we are referring to the main arches and pillars of the building, and not to the tracery of the windows, or to alterations to the walls. The two exceptions mentioned above are the pointed arches, east and west of the central tower, and the removal of the three lowest windows in the apse.

The greatest attraction to the world at large is undoubtedly **the West Front**, which is seen in its full beauty on entering the close.

The following lines, from Morris's " Earthly Paradise," may fitly introduce the subject.

" For other tales they told, and one of these
 Not all the washing of the troublous seas,
 Nor all the changeful days whereof ye know,
 Have swept from out my memory : even so
 Small things far off will be remembered clear
 When matters both more mighty and more near,
 Are waxing dim to us. I, who have seen
 So many lands, and midst such marvels been,
 Clearer than these abodes of outland men,
 Can see above the green and unburnt fen
 The little houses of an English town,
 Cross-timbered, thatched with fen-reeds coarse and brown,
 And high o'er these, three gables, great and fair,
 That slender rods of columns do upbear
 Over the minster doors, and imagery
 Of kings, and flowers no summer field doth see,
 Wrought in these gables.—Yea I heard withal,
 In the fresh morning air, the trowels fall
 Upon the stone, a thin noise far away ;
 For high up wrought the masons on that day,
 Since to the monks that house seemed scarcely well
 Till they had set a spire or pinnacle
 Each side the great porch. In that burgh I heard
 This tale, and late have set down every word
 That I remembered, when the thoughts would come
 Of what we did in our deserted home,

And of the days, long past, when we were young,
Nor knew the cloudy days that o'er us hung.
And howsoever I am now grown old,
Yet is it still the tale I then heard told
Within the guest house of that Minster Close,
Whose walls, like cliffs new made, before us rose."

It is rather a porch, or piazza, than a front; for it consists of a paved walk of some extent outside the wall of the cathedral covered at a great height by a vaulted roof which is supported by the wall and by the three great arches. Mr Fergusson, in his "Handbook of Architecture,"[1] pronounces that "as a portico, using the term in its classical sense, the west front of Peterborough is the grandest and finest in Europe": and there are few that will not agree with him. Professor Freeman says:[2]—"The portico of Peterborough is unique; the noblest conception of the old Greek translated into the speech of Christendom and of England has no fellow before it or after it." Exclusive of the spires, and the central porch and parvise, the dates of which have been given previously, the whole is of the best and purest Early English style. The effect is certainly improved by the middle arch being narrower than the others. But if the gables above had been of unequal angles, the result would have been far less satisfactory. Wisely, therefore, these angles have been made equal, and all of the same height: and the device of the architect to secure this, by making the central gable rise from points somewhat higher than the others, is admirable. It is to be observed also that the turrets, or large pinnacles, that are placed between the gables, are not placed exactly above the central line of the great piers beneath them, but are in each case a little further towards the outer arches; and it will be seen, immediately that this is pointed out, how much the upper part of the façade is thereby improved. The two great piers may be roughly taken as having for section an isosceles right-angled triangle, the right-angle being towards the west. The mouldings of the arches are supported by a series of banded shafts, six on each side of each arch. In the spaces between the shafts of the middle arch, but not of the others, are crockets for the whole height, and the innermost cavetto is entirely filled with dog-tooth ornament. All the

---

[1] "Handbook of Architecture," 2nd ed., 1859, p. 869.
[2] "English Towns and Districts," 1883, p. 29.

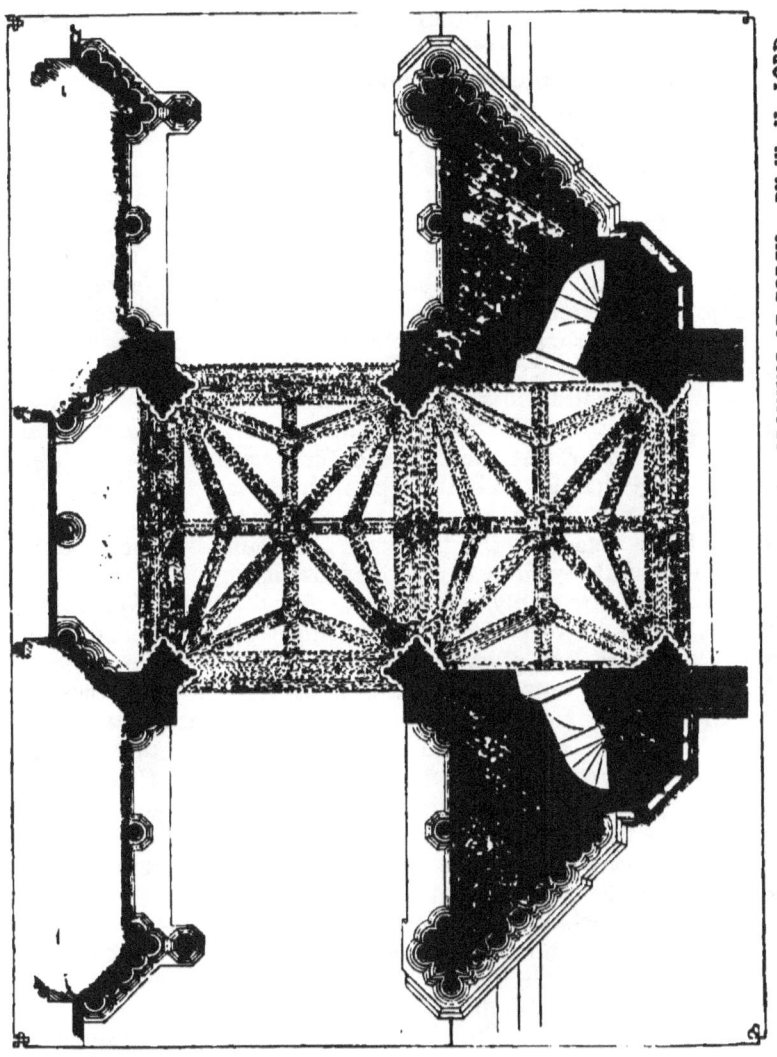

PLAN OF CENTRAL PORTION OF WEST FRONT, WITH GROINING OF PORCH, BY W. H. LORD,

shafts have floriated capitals; and the great arches have similar mouldings. Four sets of ornaments run round each arch; a continuous chevron, a richly floriated roll, a roll with bands, and a series of billets. Between the arches there rises a clustered shaft which reaches to the level of the highest points of the arches: here these shafts combine with an ornamented stringcourse which runs in a straight line along the entire front. In each of the six spandrels are a deeply recessed quatrefoil, two trefoiled arches (like the upper part of a niche), a pair of lancet-shaped niches containing figures, and a beautifully designed hexagonal ornament, with wavy edges, the cusps uniting in a central boss. The pinnacles on each side of the middle gable are at first square, then there are two octagonal stages, the uppermost pierced, and finally a short spire. The lowest stage has a double lancet with floriated capitals; the second has a lancet, also with floriated capitals, filling up each face of the octagon; the last stage has round-headed lancets, without capitals, entirely surrounded by zigzags.

The gables are richly ornamented. At the head of each is a massive cross of very fine workmanship. Along the edges of the gables are two rows of billets and the wavy ornament. Just below the crosses are three large statues, in niches of which the gable mouldings form the heads. That in the centre is S. Peter, with a mitre, the right hand uplifted in blessing, and two keys in the left hand; the other two are S. John and S. Andrew. Below plain, straight stringcourses, at the foot of these statues, are three rose windows of exceptional grace and beauty. The central one has eight spokes radiating from a flat medallion enriched with conventional foliage; these support trefoil-headed arches which have their outer mouldings thickly covered with dog-tooth; the whole is bounded by two circular bands, the inner one ornamented. The two other rose windows have six spokes instead of eight, the trefoiled arches have foliage, and the inner moulding of the bounding circles is continuously waving. The spokes in all three windows have the dog-tooth on each side. On each side of the lower part of these windows is a trefoil-headed niche containing a figure. Below these, and resting upon the long stringcourse that runs above the great arches, are sets of seven trefoil-headed niches, with a half-niche at each end. Four of these niches are pierced for windows, which have trefoils with pointed heads, though the trefoil arcading has a sub-division with round arches; and the stage above the great stringcourse has round-headed trefoils so as to be in keeping with the row of similar arches in the gables; but with these two exceptions all the arches on the arcades of the tower are pointed and without cusps. Of the spires which surmount these towers that on the south is by far the more elegant. It has pinnacles at the corners of square section, and then another set of triangular pinnacles, resting on open arches connecting the corner pinnacles with the spire. These triangular pinnacles are double the height of those at the corners. All the pinnacles and canopies over the arches have crockets. This spire is some few feet loftier than that to the north, though most measurements of the cathedral have hitherto given them as being of the same height.

The inner wall of the portico, forming the west wall of the cathedral, is covered with elaborate arcading, and so also are the ends, north and south. The designs are nearly a continuation of the arcading on the two towers. There are five lofty windows, now filled with tracery inserted in the Perpendicular period, the great west window having been enlarged at the same time. The two side doorways are exceedingly good, and should be carefully examined. The central doorway must have been of still greater beauty; but the whole of the upper part of it is hidden by the porch and parvise inserted beneath the central arch. This doorway is divided by a fine pillar rising from a well-carved base, with a very curious scene depicted on it. "It represents," writes Canon Davys,[1] "a Benedictine tortured by demons, and was doubtless intended as a significant hint to the monks that a sacred calling demands a consistent life." The portico retains its original Early English vaulting.

The **Porch** and **Parvise** beneath the middle arch was inserted, as has been previously stated, as a support to the two great piers. It is vaulted in two bays, the first being of the same dimensions as the inner width of the portico; the western bay (of the same size) thus reaches beyond the two great piers, and the corner turrets and buttresses in all project about seven feet. This gives a very substantial support to the piers. The whole composition is very fine, and quite worthy of the great portico to which it is an adjunct. It must be left to each spectator to decide for himself if it improves or diminishes the

[1] Guide, p. 48.

effect of the whole. It is of late Decorated date, highly enriched with profuse carving. The staircase turrets, as well as the great window are embattled. Possibly there may have been pinnacles now lost. The spaces north and south, and within the portico, have tracery on the walls similar to the window. The groining is very fine. One of the central bosses has a representation of the Trinity. The Father is represented as the Ancient of Days, with a Dove for the Holy Spirit above the shoulder, and the figure of the Saviour on the Cross in front. Freemasons are recommended to look for a special symbol which they alone can understand and appreciate.

The floor of the portico is paved with gravestones, some apparently in their original position. This place was at one time appropriated as a burial place for the Minor Canons.[1] Some of the stones, however, are of mediæval date, and it can be seen where the brasses have been wrenched from them: some of these have been used again for later inscriptions. One stone bears an incised cross originally filled with some coloured composition. Some of the wall-shafts have fallen and not been replaced; a few have had their place supplied by common wooden rollers, the knots in the wood being plainly discernible from the ground.

At the date of publication of this account, the full beauty of the west front cannot be appreciated, owing to the scaffolding erected in connection with the measures that are being taken to ensure its preservation. All the criticisms that have been passed upon the front, as a termination to the building, cannot be discussed here. It is clear, however, that the existence of the portico does away with any objection that could be made (as has been done with regard to the west fronts at Lincoln, Wells, and elsewhere), that the front might be considered to hide rather than to bring out the construction of the nave and aisles. It is true that the side gables are not the gables of the aisles, and indeed the roofs that are built against the gables are built only for them; but they are a legitimate finish to the great arches, and to the vaulted roof of the portico. Possibly the inequality of the great arches may be explained when we reflect that the central gable is the honest termination of the nave roof;

---

[1] Sir William Feeld, Peticanon, in his will dated 1558, desires that his body may be buried in the Gallery before the church door, where all his fellows are buried. "Gallery" here is probably a corruption of "Galilee."

the two central piers were therefore bound to be built so as to give support to the existing nave roof, and to fit it. The position of these piers being fixed, the outer ones might be as distant as was desired, for the front must of course extend to the

Photochrom Co., Ld., Photo.]
SOUTH-WEST SPIRE AND BELL-TOWER FROM THE LAUREL COURT.

entire length of the western transept. It has been commonly supposed that the three great arches of the Lincoln front suggested the idea to the Peterborough builders. If so, they improved upon their model. The central arch at Lincoln even before the round arch was altered, must have been half as high again as the side arches; and as they all are integral parts of the wall, and therefore not open, they have somewhat the appearance of magnified doorways that have been blocked up. At Snettisham, in Norfolk, is a western doorway protected by a porch with three open arches; and this has sometimes been mentioned when Peterborough west front is a subject of discussion; not, of course, as a fitting comparison, but as an illustration of the architectural method employed. At Snettisham, however, the porch is a small erection even for the church to which it gives entrance, and does not nearly extend to the entire width of the building.

The following is the quaint description given in "Magna Britannia," published 1724:—" The western Front is very Noble and Majestick of Columel Work, and supported by three such tall Arches, as England can scarcely shew the like, which are adorned with a great Variety of curious Imagery. The Form of Arches is by the modern Architects called, The Bull's Eye, not Semicircular. The whole is one of the noblest pieces of Gothick Building in England."

The Bell-tower, that rises from the western transept, and is seen above and beyond the north gable of the front, is a little later than the front itself. It is of good workmanship, and quite in keeping with the older part. There are rows of lancets in the belfry stage, and the four corner pinnacles are very similar to the large pinnacles that are placed between the gables of the front, but all the lancets are pointed, and there are little gables above each. This tower was once surmounted by a wooden spire. When this was erected does not seem to be known. It was not of particularly graceful design, judging from views of the cathedral taken when it was standing. It was removed in the early part of the present century.

Passing round to the north side of the cathedral we are at once struck with the beauty of the termination of the western transept. The arcading on the north side of the tower of the front is identical with that on the west side; but to the east there is only arcading in the three upper stages. Mr Paley's remarks upon the great windows of the western transept may be quoted. He says[1] they "deserve particular examination,

[1] Paley, p. 30.

WEST PORCH AND PARVISE.   DRAWN BY W. H. LORD.

heads of the niches themselves are round at the top. The three intervening niches contain figures. All these nine figures have a nimbus; and as these, with the three under the crosses, make up twelve, it is assumed that they represent the Apostles. The six smaller statues, just above, are said to be kings; the twelve below, benefactors. There are thus thirty statues in all, and most were no doubt carved at the time of the erection of

IRON GATES TO WEST PORCH. DRAWN BY O. R. ALLBROW.

the front; but two or three appear to be of earlier date, and may possibly have formed part of the embellishments of the Saxon church.

The Towers north and south, up to the height of the parapets, are of the same date as the portion already described. They are ornamented with blank arcading in six stages, of different dimensions and character; all is in perfect harmony with the rest of the composition. The loftiest of the stages of this

WEST FRONT OF PETERBOROUGH CATHEDRAL, RESTORED ACCORDING TO GUNTON, A.D. 1780.

not only because they are very early and fine specimens of cusped and traceried windows—indeed, among the best in the kingdom—but for a remarkable peculiarity in the jambs; whereof one side is Norman, with the square capitals to the jamb-shafts both within and without, and the other Early English, as are the arch-mouldings and hoods round the whole arches, which were probably semicircular at first, for at present the point cuts through a stringcourse inside. The frames of the entire windows are later work, having no attachment or bonding to the jambs, as is clearly manifested to the eye." These windows rise as high as the top of those of the triforium. Above is a round-headed window with a slightly smaller arch on each side, with cushion capitals. The gable itself is designedly made to resemble one of the gables of the west front. It is surmounted by a cross, and bordered by the wavy ornament; it has a rose window; and beneath is an arcade of five round-headed trefoiled arches supported by shafts, having at the inner wall three lancet windows. The circular window is without tracery; it has twelve cusps. At each side of the gable is a pinnacle, almost a copy of those on the front, except that the lowest stage is here octagonal instead of square.

On the north side of the nave is a single door, now called **the Dean's door**, of good Norman work. On each side are three shafts with cushion capitals slightly ornamented; and in the round arches above are different mouldings of the style. The windows to the aisle, ten in number, are very broad, of five lights each, under depressed arches. The tracery and mouldings indicate that these were substituted for the original windows towards the close of the thirteenth century. At the same time it would seem that the walls above, in the triforium range, were heightened, because the parapet at the top is of Early English work, although the three-light windows beneath it are Decorated, and were not inserted until the next century. At the foot of the triforium range is the original Norman arcade of round-headed arches: below the existing Decorated windows is now a blank space of wall, where at first was the Norman window, rising somewhat higher than the arcade. What the original arrangement was can be seen on the east side of the north transept. The Norman clerestory range has been altered only by having Perpendicular tracery put in the windows,

THE CATHEDRAL—EXTERIOR. 51

and by the addition of a Decorated parapet. The original corbel-table was allowed to remain.

The Lantern-tower has on each face two large windows

THE DEAN'S DOOR, NORTH SIDE OF NAVE.   DRAWN BY H. P. CLIFFORD.

with transoms, of three lights. The tracery is that known as nettracery. Between these windows is a blank window, if the term may be allowed; the tracery exists, but there never was a window; this is of four lights; while between the windows and the corner turrets are similar traceries of two lights. The whole is surmounted by a parapet above a plain arcade. The corner turrets are octangular. As at present finished at the top there is undoubtedly an appearance of their being incomplete.

The west side of the **North Transept** is a very excellent specimen of Norman work; and we find less change here than in any other part of the cathedral that belongs to the same period. The tracery of the windows is Perpendicular, but the windows themselves are otherwise unaltered: at the top of all is a Decorated parapet, which is here composed of a series of quatrefoils; and the parapet to the corner turrets is not Norman. As there is no aisle on the west side of this transept, there has been no alteration in the wall, as was the case with the nave aisles.

The north end of the transept is similar; but the shallow buttresses between the windows rise to a greater height, and there is another arcade above the upper tier of windows, and a blank arch in the gable. The gable has crockets, and a cross at the apex. The lower Norman window in the aisle here is unlike any others on this side of the church, but there are four others like it on the south. The upper aisle window here is of three lights, with a large pointed trefoil above them instead of tracery.

The east wall of this transept is specially worthy of note. We can trace the lines of the roof of the Lady Chapel which formerly stood to the east of the wall; and beneath this are two bays of the original triforium range, unaltered except that the windows are filled in. Between these and the roof are six Early English lancets. Below are the upper parts of the two great arches which were constructed as an entrance to the Lady Chapel. When the Lady Chapel was pulled down in the seventeenth century these were converted into windows filled with late tracery in imitation of Perpendicular work, and the lower part was walled up, except that a doorway was constructed. This was afterwards blocked up for many years, and only reopened during the recent restoration works. The same alteration has been effected in the western part of the choir aisle, the arches towards the Lady Chapel having been in like manner made into windows. The lower window nearest the tower is a very graceful geometric window of three lights, exactly like the three in the south transept; the window above is of the same

S. B. Bolas & Co., Photo.]
THE APSE AND NEW BUILDING, FROM THE SOUTH-EAST.

period as all the other Decorated windows of the triforium range.

Between the Lady Chapel and the north aisle of the choir was a passage (to which the two great arches were open), and at the eastern end of it was a small vaulted chapel, the remains of which are clearly to be seen, including the broken piscina. Above this were chambers, concerning which Gunton[1] has preserved a tradition that they were "the habitation of a devout Lady, called Agnes, or Dame Agnes, out of whose Lodging-Chamber there was a hole made askew in the window walled up, having its prospect just upon the altar of the Ladies Chappel, and no more. It seems she was devout in her generation, that she chose this place for her retirement, and was desirous that her eyes, as well as ears, might wait upon her publick Devotions." He says also that little is known of her except that she was a benefactress to the church, and that a wood she bestowed upon it is still called by her name.

At the extreme east is the **New Building**. Its side walls are built in continuation of the walls of the choir aisles, and it has a square end. It is lit by eleven large windows, all of the same design, of which the five at the east end, and the two most western of the sides, are of four lights each, the remaining four having three lights each. Between each pair of the latter there is no buttress; there are thus in all twelve buttresses, six being at the east end. These are massive, having to support the heavy fan-tracery within. Each buttress has a seated figure at the top, commonly believed to represent an Apostle; but the outlines are much worn, and it is not possible to distinguish them by any symbols they may bear. There is a very handsome open parapet, adorned with ornaments and shields bearing letters or monograms.

The parapet of quatrefoils, which runs round the sides of the transepts and choir, is not continued in the apse; an Early English parapet, with five circular medallions cusped, having been erected previously. The Decorated windows of the apse are particularly fine. The arcade beneath the upper tier, unlike the arcade in similar positions in other parts of the church, is here intersecting.

The three beautiful geometric windows in the east wall of the **South Transept,** which have three circles in the heads with

[1] Gunton, p. 91.

five cusps, are most likely of exactly the same design as the windows in the demolished Lady Chapel. At the south end of this transept is a Norman door, and outside are the remains of a short covered passage which communicated with the cloisters. These will be described hereafter.

The south side of the nave differs only from the north side in its having two doorways from the cloisters, in the superior elegance of the south-west spire, and in the unfinished state of the south-west tower. The portion of this tower above the roof Mr Paley pronounces, from the details of the windows on the east side, to be of much later date than the other tower; and he adds that it is hard to see how the roof of the transept was terminated before this stage was built to abut it. Both towers are longer from east to west than from north to south.

CHAPTER III.

THE CATHEDRAL—INTERIOR.

THE plan of the **Monastery** here given has been taken from one prepared by the late Precentor Walcott of Chichester, and communicated to "The Building News," in 1878. In this plan the choir is represented as it was arranged in olden times, and not as it appeared after it was shortened by the erection of the organ-screen under the eastern arch of the tower in Dean Monk's time. The position of the ancient buildings is also indicated, though some of them, as the Lady Chapel, Dormitory, Chapter-house and Infirmary Chapel, have long been destroyed. The various portions will be understood by the following references.

(1) New Building. (2) Reredos, or Altar-screen. (3) Screens. Recent discoveries have proved that the choir aisles originally ended, or at least were designed to end, in apses. (4) High Altar. (5) Entry to passage to Lady Chapel; a small chapel to the east. (6) Lady Chapel. (7) Door to it from north transept aisle. (8) Chapel of S. John. (9) Chapel of S. James. (10) Chapel of S. Oswald, the Holy Trinity Chapel above it. (11) Chapel of S. Benedict. (12) Chapel of SS. Kyneburga and Kyneswitha, sisters of Peada and Wulfere, the original founders of the monastery. (13) Choir. (14) Sacristy. (15) Choir-screen. (16) Front of rood-loft. (17) Nave. (18) Gate to grave-yard. (19) Gate to Prior's lodging. (20) Minster close. (21) Gatehouse to Abbot's lodging, with the Knights' chamber above. (22) Chancel of the chapel of S. Thomas of Canterbury. (23) Great gateway of the close. (24, 25) Doorways from the cloisters. (26) Slype. (27) Parlour. (28) Chapter-house. (29) Porch. (30) Dormitory. (31) Cloisters. (32) Lavatory. (33) Refectory. (34) Dark entry. (35) Gong-

(36) Kitchen. (37) Abbot's lodging. (38) Prior's lodging.
(39) Infirmarer's hall. (40) Chapel to Infirmary, dedicated to
S. Laurence. (41) The chancel, and (42) the nave of this
chapel. (43) Hall of Infirmary, the inmates occupying the
aisles. (44) Door to Infirmary. (45) Precinct wall and

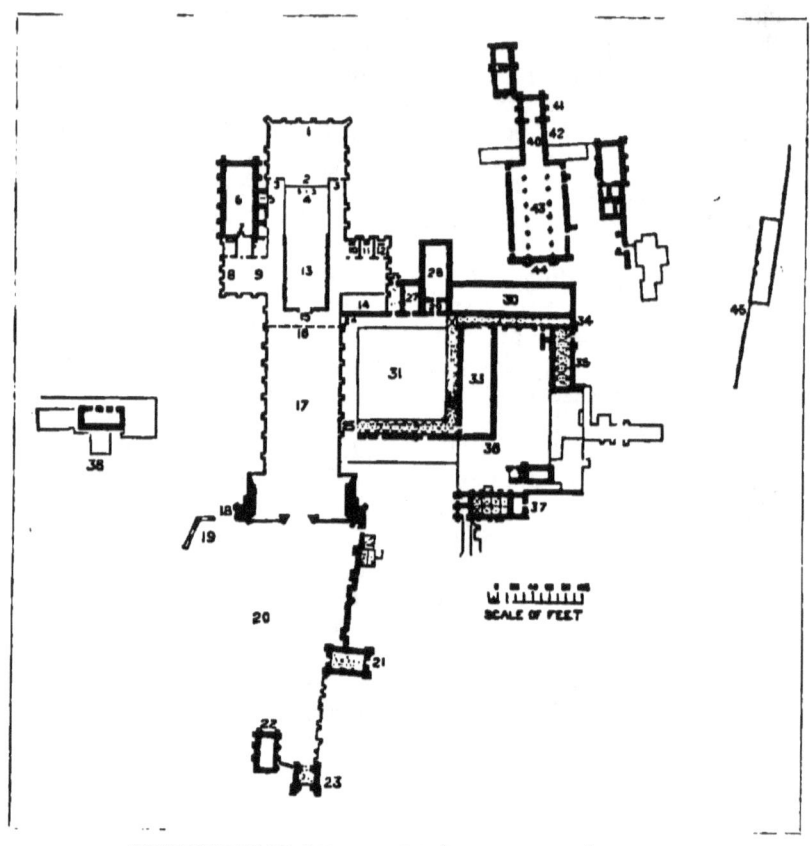

PETERBOROUGH MONASTERY (BENEDICTINE). FROM
"THE BUILDING NEWS," 1878.

stables. The building to the south of the Infirmary, not
numbered in this plan, is an ancient residence now occupied
by the Archdeacon of Northampton, Bishop of Leicester. The
small building south-west of the front is an old vaulted room,

now used as a clerk's office, originally believed to have been the Penitentiary. The old abbey gaol has escaped notice, though it in part remains. Its door is immediately to the right upon entering the close through the great gateway.

The Interior.—With few exceptions, to be noticed in due course, the whole of the interior of the cathedral is in the Norman style, and many judge it to be the most perfect specimen in England. The plan consists of a nave of ten bays, with aisles, and a western transept; transepts of four bays with eastern chapels, the south transept having also a groined chamber to the west, extending for its whole length; a choir of four bays, terminating in an apse, nearly semicircular, with aisles; and beyond the apse a large square-ended addition for more chapels, having a groined stone roof of fan tracery, now known as the New Building. The ritual choir, as distinguished from the architectural choir, extends two bays into the nave. This arrangement is a return to the ancient one used by the Benedictines, the choir in Dean Monk's alterations having been limited to the portion east of the central tower.

As we enter at the west door we see at a glance the entire length, and the whole beauty of the admirable proportion of the several parts. While many may wish that the great arches of the tower which can be seen from the west end had never been altered from the round form of the Norman builders, few will regret that the Decorated arches which took their place were retained when the tower was rebuilt, instead of having new arches in the Norman style substituted. The want of colour which is so marked a defect in many English cathedrals is not so conspicuous here, because of the painted ceiling.

The Norman work being in the main so complete, it will be best to begin the description where the building itself was begun, at the apse. At the west door we stand where the work was finished. We know when the building commenced, in 1117, but we do not know exactly when the whole was finished to the western wall; but, speaking roughly, though not very far from the truth, we may say that the minster took eighty years to complete. This may be slightly more than was actually taken. During that time the work was not continuous: there were some Abbots who appear to have done little or nothing towards extending the works, and sometimes accordingly there was an entire cessation from active operations. Including the west front, we should have to assign nearly 120 years to the completion of the building.

The Choir.—Up to the commencement of the apse the choir is of four bays. The pillars are alternately round and with ten or twelve sides; all have cushioned capitals, indented to agree with the mouldings above; all had a shaft on the inner side rising to the roof, to support the wooden groining, but the lower parts of some of these shafts were cut away to make room for the woodwork of Dean Monk's choir. The ornamentation throughout is plentiful, but we see nothing but the billet, the chevron, and the hatchet moulding, all indicative of early work. The triforium has two recessed arches, beneath the principal arch, divided by a plain shaft. It is specially to be noticed that all the tympana in the triforium range are differently ornamented. In each bay of the clerestory range are three arches, one large and two small ones; the capitals to the shafts have the plain cushion (as in the triforium) and from these shafts a narrower arch connects them with the outer wall. There is a passage here all round the choir. Below the triforium a stringcourse of chevrons runs all along.

Between the choir bays and the apse is solid wall, rather longer than the distance between the central lines of adjoining piers. Here are two massive half-pillars, reaching to the roof, undoubtedly meant to be crowned with a round arch like those to the transepts; and this seems to shew that the intention was to vault the apse with stone. The apse is by far the best large Norman apse remaining in this country. At Norwich, where is the only possible rival, the lower part only is semicircular and original, the whole of the upper part being of Decorated date, and pentagonal. This apse is in five divisions, separated by clustered shafts which rise to the roof. Originally there were three tiers of round-headed Norman windows; the nine windows in the centre were enlarged and filled with very good tracery in the Decorated period, and the lower windows also on the other two sides. When, in the Perpendicular age, the new building was added, the three lowest windows were removed altogether and the wall beneath them, leaving three open arches. The inner wall surface of the five lowest windows has been filled with elegant hanging tracery of fourteenth century date, the designs being all different. In some cases this tracery is placed just below the Norman stringcourse, but in others the string-

THE CHOIR, LOOKING EAST.

[Photochrom Co., Ltd., Photo.]

course has been removed to make room for it. There was no necessity to convert the two lowest side windows into arches; and they accordingly remain there to this day; but being no

Photochrom Co., Ld., Photo.]

VIEW FROM TRIFORIUM SOUTH OF CHOIR.

longer exposed to the outer air all the glass is gone, though the notches that held it, and the strong bars that protected it, have been suffered to stay. There was never any ambulatory round the apse outside; we can still see, from the new building, portions of a stringcourse which was external, as well as other evidences that the apse was the end of the church. It is also known that there was a highway at the east end of the church, almost touching it. In the stage corresponding to the triforium are to be seen on the walls the remains of painted coats of arms, the shape of the shield suggesting that they are as early as the thirteenth century; some also have been cut in half by the later Decorated alterations.

The choir roof is vaulted in wood. In the time of Dean Saunders it was repainted with gold and colours. From the character of the bosses, and the capitals where the wood is joined to the tall shafts rising from the pillars in the choir, and from the general ornamentation, it is manifest that this was constructed towards the end of the fifteenth century. It was at one time painted all over yellow and white. The carving of the different bosses is well worth attention. There has not been discovered any mark or initials that might help us to assign a positive date. We can see, among other designs, the cross keys of the patron Saint; the Saviour on the Cross accompanied by S. Mary and S. John (this is in the central line, near the tower); three lilies; three fishes with intersecting tails. The roof over the apse is flat. It has been decorated from a design by Sir G. G. Scott, with an emblematical representation of Christ as a Vine, the Disciples being half-figures in medallions among the foliage. An inscription bearing upon the subject forms the border. The general effect will be like, though not identical with, the original painting in this place. This was one of the decorations of the church that excited the fury of the soldiers and others who dismantled the minster in the civil war in the seventeenth century. "This is the Idol they worship and adore" was the cry of some of the party; upon which muskets were discharged, and the picture wholly defaced. The description of the design is given in these words:[1] "Over this place" (that is, the altar-screen) "in the Roof of the Church, in a large Oval yet to be seen, was the Picture of our Saviour seated on a Throne, one hand erected, and holding a Globe in the other: attended with the four Evangelists and Saints on each side, with Crowns in their hands; intended, I suppose, for a Representation of our Saviour's coming to judgment."

[1] Patrick's Supplement to Gunton, p. 334.

S. B. Bolas & Co., Photo.]
NORTH TRANSEPT AND MORNING CHAPEL.

The flat roof of the apse being lower than the roof of the choir, the space between the levels is filled with twelve painted figures.

The whole of the internal fittings of the choir (speaking now of the ritual choir) are new, and are part of the recent restoration. The new woodwork began to be placed in position in 1890. There is indeed a little old work, which was in the old choir before it was altered in the early part of this century. When removed, some of the front desks had been placed in the morning chapel, though much of the projecting tracery work was taken off. It was realised, when the existing stall-work was being designed, that these would be very suitable for use in their old position. Accordingly, all that could be so used have been placed again in the choir, with their traceried panels restored ; and the new work is made of the same character. The **New Stalls** are of the finest oak, with miserere seats ; the backs have rich tracery, with raised shields, moulded groined ceilings, and carved bosses at the intersection of the ribs. They are surmounted by octagonal canopies, in three stages, the uppermost containing a niche for a carved figure to each stall, while other figures, of much smaller size, are to be seen below. A few have at the back the armorial bearings of the donor, or some other symbol, such as the masonic emblems in those given by the Freemasons of England. The names of the cathedral officers and others to whom the different stalls are assigned, have been inscribed on the label at the head of each ; and it is intended on each to record the donor's name.

With the exception of the first figure, the whole of the larger figures at the top of the canopies have some special connection with the monastery or the cathedral. Beginning at the Dean's stall, and proceeding eastwards, the statues on the south side represent the following :—

Two at the summit of the Dean's stall, SS. Paul and Andrew.

1. S. Peter, the Patron Saint.
2. Saxulf (656), the first Abbot.
3. Adulf (971), Abbot, afterwards Archbishop of York.
4. Kenulf (992), Abbot, afterwards Bishop of Winchester.
5. Leofric (1057), Abbot.
6. Turold (1069), Abbot, appointed by William the Conqueror.

7. Ernulf (1107), Abbot, afterwards Bishop of Rochester.
8. Martin de Bec (1133), Abbot when the choir was dedicated.
9. Benedict (1175), Abbot. He built the greater part, if not all, of the nave.
10. Martin of Ramsey (1226), Abbot.
11. John of Calais (1249), Abbot. He built the infirmary, probably the refectory, and part of the cloisters.
12. Richard of London (1274), Abbot. He built the north-western tower.
13. Adam of Boothby (1321), Abbot.
14. William Genge (1396), first mitred Abbot.
15. Richard Ashton (1438), Abbot. He began the new building.
16. Robert Kirton (1496), Abbot. He finished the new building, and built the Deanery gateway.
17. John Towers (1638), Bishop. Previously Dean (1630).
18. Thomas White (1685), Bishop. Nonjuror.
19. William Connor Magee (1868), Bishop, afterwards Archbishop of York.
20. Simon Patrick (1679), Dean, afterwards Bishop of Chichester, and finally of Ely.
21. Augustus Page Saunders (1853), Dean.
22. John James Stewart Perowne (1878), Dean, now Bishop of Worcester.

The upper figures on the north side are these:—

Two at the summit of the Vice-Dean's stall, Kings Wolfere and Ethelred.[1]

1. Peada, King of Mercia, founder of the monastery.
2. Cuthbald (675), second Abbot.
3. Edgar, King of Mercia and Wessex, restorer of the monastery.
4. Ethelfleda, his queen.
5. Brando (1066), Abbot.
6. Hereward, the Saxon patriot (1070), nephew of Abbot Brando, and knighted by him.
7. John de Sais (1114), Abbot. He commenced the building of the existing choir.

---

[1] King Ethelred resigned his crown and became Abbot of Bardney. He is here figured with a mitre.

8. Hedda (died 870), Abbot, murdered by the Danes.

9. Robert of Lindsey (1214), Abbot. He holds a model of the west front, probably built or begun in his time.

10. Godfrey of Crowland (1299), Abbot. He bears a model of the gateway to the palace grounds.

11. William Ramsey (1471), Abbot. He was one of the donors of the brass eagle lectern still in use.

12. William Parys (died 1286), Prior. He built the Lady Chapel.

13. S. Giles, the famous Benedictine Abbot, with his tame hind beside him.

14. Hugo Candidus, the chronicler.

15. Henry of Overton (1361), Abbot.

16. Queen Katherine of Arragon.

17. John Cosin (1640), Dean, afterwards Bishop of Durham.

18. Simon Gunton (1646), Prebendary, the historian of the church.

19. Herbert Marsh (1819), Bishop.

20. George Davys (1839), Bishop.

21. James Henry Monk (1822), Dean, afterwards Bishop of Gloucester and Bristol.

22. Marsham Argles (1891), Dean. Previously Canon (1849).

The dates in the above lists, unless stated otherwise, are the dates of appointment. With the single exception of Henry of Overton, of whom very little indeed is known except that he was abbot for nearly thirty years, the selection that has been made appears to be very good. In some way or other all the persons represented are eminent. The authorities are to be congratulated upon their including in the series several dignitaries of the present century.

The smaller figures on the south side are all characters from the New Testament; those on the north side are taken from the Old Testament. The carving on the sides of the two westernmost stalls is of great interest. The panels on the south represent the miraculous preservation of the arm of S. Oswald. This arm was one of the greatest treasures of the house, and was reputed to be the cause of many cures. The legend is given hereafter in the notice of Abbot Elsinus, the great collector of relics. In the corresponding position on the north side is represented the story of S. Ethelwold, Bishop of Winchester.

This has been already related in the historical section. The litany desk is a piece of excellent work : it is placed midway between the seats of the choristers.

The carving on the **Pulpit** and **Throne** will repay careful study. In the niches at the base of the pulpit are four abbots, chiefly connected with the erection of the building. They are John de Sais, who holds a model of the apse, Martin de Bec, William of Waterville, and Walter of S. Edmunds. Round the main body of the pulpit are four saints in niches, SS. Peter, Paul, John and James, each easily identified by what is held in the hand. Between these niches are wide panels carved with subjects associated with preaching. Abbot Saxulf preaching to the Mercians; Christ sending forth the Apostles; S. Peter preaching after the descent of the Holy Spirit at Pentecost.

The throne is raised on three steps. Above the canopy is a lofty spire. On the sides of the seat are SS. Peter and Paul. On the book board are symbolical representations of the virtues of Temperance, Wisdom, Fortitude, and Justice. In the lower tier on the canopy are six figures : Saxulf, first Abbot ; Cuthwin, first Bishop of Leicester ; John de Sais ; Benedict ; S. Hugh, Bishop of Lincoln, his hand resting on the head of his tame swan ; and John Chambers, last Abbot and first Bishop of Peterborough. In the upper tier are four Bishops : Bishop Dove, the theologian ; Bishop Cumberland, the philosopher ; Bishop Kennett, the antiquary ; and Archbishop Magee, the orator.

One of the statues over the stalls, that representing S. Giles, has also a figure of a hind ; in the representation of S. Hugh of Lincoln on the pulpit we see a swan. The hind was really a type of solitude and purity of life, and as such is found in many ancient carvings and paintings accompanying various Saints. There is also a legend specially connecting this creature with S. Giles. In a retreat in a forest in the diocese of Nismes, the recluse, with one companion, is said to have lived on the fruits of the earth and the milk of a hind. Some dogs that were out hunting pursued this hind, and she took refuge in the dwelling of the Saint. The sportsman, Flavius Wamba, King of the Goths, treated him with every mark of respect, and gave him land wherewith to endow a monastery. Of S. Hugh's swan a long account is given in the " Vita S. Hugonis Lincolniensis " published in the Rolls Series. A swan never before seen at the place flew to the Bishop at his manor at Stowe directly after he had been enthroned at Lincoln. He became passionately

[*Photochrom Co., Ld., Photo.*]

THE PULPIT.

attached to the bishop, but exhibited no liking for any one else. He considered himself bound to protect his master, driving other people away from him, "As I myself," writes Giraldus

Cambrensis, "have often with wonder seen," with his wings and beak. In this way he was somewhat of a nuisance to the bishop's household, for no one dared to go near the bishop when he was resting, for fear of the swan. In the bishop's absence a keeper attended to the bird, and was allowed to feed him, but the swan would suffer no fondling. He survived the bishop for many years.

The new Organ is the gift of an anonymous donor. His name is of course known to those that are in the confidence of the authorities, but it is not the donor's wish that it should be publicly given. He is not a resident of Peterborough. This organ has been built by Hill & Son, at a cost (including the case) of £4,400. The action is tubular pneumatic, the wind being supplied by a gas engine. The Pedal (with the exception of two stops, Bourdon and Bass Flute), Great Solo and Swell Organs, are placed in four bays of the triforium on the north side; the Choir Organ and two pedal stops above named are in the first bay of the north aisle beyond the stalls. The Console is in the second bay of the aisle. The organ comprises 68 stops and 4,453 pipes.

The Canopied Reredos or Baldachino was given by the eight surviving children of Dean Saunders as a memorial of their parents. The retable was given by the Old Boys of the King's School. The reredos is a magnificent erection, and renders the east end of this cathedral one of the most dignified in the kingdom. The daïs on which it stands is thirteen feet square, and the summit reaches to the height of thirty-five feet. Four large marble columns stand at the corners, from the capitals of which spring cusped arches, the spandrels being enriched with mosaic; while at the angles, above the columns, are figures of the Evangelists in niches. The large central panel in front has the figure of Our Lord; at the back is S. Peter. The material is Derbyshire alabaster; the work was executed by Mr Robert Davison, of London.

The Mosaic Pavement, also the work of Mr Davison, was the gift of the late Dean and Miss Argles. The following description of it is from the pen of Mr Davison.

" Passing into the choir from the west, the pavement between the stalls is of tesselated Roman mosaic, in an effective geometrical pattern of squares, and oblongs of red, green and white marbles. The first bay of the chancel is also in Roman mosaic, but of more elaborate design, the central portion being a framework of interlacing cream bands, forming diamond shaped panels alternating with circles, the centres of these panels being varied reds and greens ; the framework surrounds four large panels of Pavonazzo d' Italie, each in six slabs. This is a beautiful marble of feathery purple grey veinings on a creamy white ground. This central part is flanked on each side by a broad band of the same Pavonazzo, which separates it from the large side panels of a bold design of squares of red, green and cream placed diagonally, interlaced by white bands ;

Photochrom Co., Ld., Photo.]

APSE AND CANOPIED REREDOS.

upon these panels stand the pulpit on the north side, and the bishop's throne on the south. This bay is approached from the choir by the first marble step which is in Frosterley, a marble with beautiful madrepores of light colour on a dark ground. The next bay is of similar design to the first, but is approached by two steps of Levanto marble of reddish brown tint with small veinings of white. The third and fourth bays are in a marble mosaic called *Opus Alexandrinum*, composed of various rich marbles of brilliant reds, greens, greys, yellows, and creams, divided into the main design by bands of Pavonazzo. The design of the third bay is divided into three equal panels, in the centre of which are four large slabs of Cipolino, a charming marble of a light green tint in broad wavy lines on a lighter ground, which are framed in by a combination of small panels of mosaic of varied rich patterns of triangles and squares, which are again enclosed by a broad border of mosaic of white squares on a ground of light green Vert de Suède. The step up to this bay, and also the step to the next and to the altar pace, all of which stretch the full length of the chancel, as well as the three steps to the altar daïs, are in carefully selected Pavonazzo. The design of the fourth bay is a system of interlacing bands, forming alternately large and small octagons, between which are squares and oblongs. The small octagons are rich plaques of marble, while the large ones are divided radially into eight panels. All these parts are filled with mosaic of varying patterns and colours. At each end of this bay is a long panel of overlapping circles, filled in with rich mosaic. The panel on the altar pace and the three panels on the altar daïs are in the same mosaic, each of a different design; the long plaques of marble in the upper panel are red and green of rich dark marbles. The two panels at the side of the daïs are in opus sectile, a design of hexagons of Pavonazzo, with diamonds of Vert des Alpes between them. The broad band of red, the whole length of the chancel on the outsides of the pavement, is of Levanto marble, forming a finish to the work."

The Screens, enclosing the four eastern bays of the choir, were given as a public memorial to Dean Argles. They are of very admirable wrought-iron. The same may be said of the choir gates. The former are the work of White & Son, of London; the latter of Singer & Son, of Frome. The short pillars that support the choir gates, and the unrelieved backs of the returned stalls, have at present the unsatisfactory appearance of all unfinished work. A drawing of the complete design is exhibited in a frame on an adjacent pillar.

The single ancient object among the fittings in the choir is the brass eagle **Lectern.** This was given to the monastery by William Ramsey, Abbot, and John Malden, Prior; it is consequently of late fifteenth century date. An inscription record ing the names of the donors, in two Latin lines, was engraved round a projection in the middle of the stem. Centuries of hard scouring have obliterated this; but the upper and lower ends of most of the letters can just be traced. An expert can satisfy himself that the inscription as preserved by Gunton is practically correct. It seems to have been this, though it is not possible to vouch for every letter.

Hæc tibi lectrina dant Petre metallica bina
Johēs Malden prior et Wills de Ramiseya.

Besides the donors already named, the following became contributors for special objects, many of them having in addition given substantial assistance in money to the restoration fund. The choir pulpit, Bishop's throne, and the cost of cleaning the whitewash from the nave were given by Dean Argles. Enlargement of foot-pace, and extension of mosaic pavement, by Mrs Argles. Decoration of ceiling of lantern tower, and new frames for the bells, by Mr H. P. Gates, Chapter Clerk. Litany desk, by Mrs Rigg. Altar ornaments, by Canon Alderson. The 44 stalls were given by Archbishop Magee, Lady Elizabeth Villiers (7), Lady Louisa Wells, Mr H. P. Gates, Friends of Canon Clayton, Family of Canon Pratt, Hon. Canon Willes, Hon. Canon Twells, an ex-chorister of the cathedral, Mr James Bristow, Mr. W. U. Heygate, Mr S. G. Stopford-Sackville, Mrs Yard, Mr J. D. Goodman, Miss Pears, Mrs Perry Herrick, Mrs W. L. Collins and Mrs H. L. Mansel, Mr Albert Pell, Mrs Dawson Rowley, The Mayor and Corporation, Mr F. James, the Freemasons of England (3), Friends of Lady Isham and Miss Perowne (2), Rev. W. R. P. Waudby, Mr G. L. Watson, Major-General Sotheby, Mrs Hunt, Rev. A. Redifer, Mr J. G. Dearden, Mrs Percival, the Misses Broughton, Rev. S. A. T. Yates (in memory of Mr Charles Davys Argles), Rev W. H. Cooper, Mr T. A. Argles, Mrs Argles.

The choir aisles are vaulted; the section of the vaulting ribs is much heavier than in the aisles of the nave, and shews an earlier date. It has recently been discovered that these aisles, contrary to what was usually believed, were terminated with apses and were not square-ended. In the south aisle is traced on the floor the position of the old semi-circular ending. The windows here were altered at the same time as those in the nave aisles; but in the north choir aisle the windows were taken out and arches formed leading to the passage between this aisle and the Lady Chapel, the most western arch being Perpendicular: in the seventeenth century, when the Lady Chapel was pulled down, these arches were again filled up with masonry and windows. The third window in this aisle has escaped alteration in form; but Perpendicular tracery has been inserted.

The eastern ends of both aisles were altered in Early English times. They have now a groined roof of one bay of that period, and very handsome double piscinas. The aumbry on the north side in the south choir aisle has been glazed, and is utilised as a cupboard to hold some curiosities. In the north choir aisle there is an approach to the morning chapel through a screen; but in the south choir aisle the corresponding space is filled by a Norman monumental arch.

The New Building built beyond the apse is a very noble specimen of late Perpendicular work. It was begun by Abbot Richard Ashton (1438–1471), and completed by Abbot Robert Kirton (1496–1528): the works seem to have been suspended between these periods. The roof has the beautiful fan tracery, very similar on a smaller scale to that at King's College Chapel at Cambridge. The building is of the width of the choir and aisles together. It contained three altars at the date of the suppression of monasteries, "upon each altar a Table of the Passion of Christ, Gilt."

The central bay has been recently fitted up for early celebrations of the Holy Communion. The junction of this addition with the original Norman apse is admirable, and should be specially noticed. Parts of the original external stringcourse of the apse can be seen. The ornamentation on the bosses of the roof, and in the cavetto below the windows, and round the great arches from the choir aisles, is very varied. It must be sufficient here to indicate some of the designs. Most need little explanation, but a few are hard to understand. On the roof may be seen the three lions of England, a cross between four martlets, three crowns each pierced by an arrow, and another design. The smaller designs include four-leaved flowers, Tudor roses, fleurs-de-lys, the portcullis, some undescribable creatures, crossed keys, crossed swords, crossed crosiers, crosses, crowns, crowns pierced with arrows, crowned female heads, an eagle, the head of the Baptist in a charger, an angel, mitres, three feathers rising from a crown, S. Andrew's cross, and perhaps others. There are also some rebuses, and some lettering. On the north wall, in six several squares, are the letters of the name Ashton interwoven with scrolls; the letters AR before a church, and a bird on a tun occur more than once. This certainly refers to Abbot Robert Kirton; but what the bird means is not clear. In the moulding over the large arch to the south choir aisle are four sets of letters. They form the last verse of the psalter. The words are contracted: they stand for *Omnis spiritus laudet Dominum.*

The Transepts, including the arch to the aisles, are of four bays, and, as has before been pointed out, are of precisely the same character as the work in the choir. The central piers here are octagonal. All round the Norman portion of the church, below the windows, is an arcade of round arches with simple round mouldings and plain cushion capitals: in the choir and transepts these have not intersecting heads, as in the nave. The western sides of the transepts have no piers or triforium, but a passage runs along in front of the windows in the triforium range. The chapels to the east have Perpendicular screens. In the north transept those three chapels were made into one which was used for early service, and called the morning chapel. We read in the chapter records of a minor canon being appointed to read the prayers at 6 o'clock, and once at least the hour is named as 5 o'clock, in the morning. This chapel was fitted up with some of the desks from the choir; and, judging from a number of names and initials that had been cut upon the desks, it has been conjectured that it was at one time used for the chapel of the King's School. At the north end is a desk for the reader or readers made out of two Early English stalls; there are three double shafts with admirably carved wooden foliage in the capitals. A very fine little Norman door leads to the staircase to the triforium. It should be mentioned that in the triforium is arranged an excellent series of stones, fragments, mouldings, and various ornaments, found in different places during the recent restoration. On the east wall are hung two large pieces of tapestry, representing scenes from the early chapters of the Acts of the Apostles, of no special merit. In all probability these were once in the choir. One window in the north transept aisle and all three in the south have fine geometrical tracery. The three chapels in the south transept were used as vestries until a few years ago, when the space be-

[*Photochrom Co., Ld., Photo.*]
THE NEW BUILDING FROM THE SOUTH-WEST.

neath the bell-tower and part of the north aisle of the nave was converted into a large vestry for both clergy and choir. In the chapel here nearest the choir there remains the lower part of the newel staircase which led to an upper chapel. On the west side of the south transept has been erected a building which has in its time served many different purposes. It can hardly be called an aisle, as there is only access to the transept by a single ogee-headed doorway, which is a Decorated insertion. This building is of late, almost transition, Norman date;

Photochrom Co., Ld., Photo.]

THE TRANSEPTS, LOOKING NORTH.

and is not very many years later than the transept itself. It can be seen from the cloister court that it had originally three gables. The roof is vaulted. In an inventory of goods made in 1539, printed in Gunton, there is one chapel described as the "Ostrie Chapel," which is believed to refer to this building. In a plan drawn in Bishop Kennett's time and dedicated to him, the south part is called "The Hostry Chapel, now the Chapter-House," and the north part is called the "Chapel of St. Sprite or the Holy Ghost." In some plans it is called the vestry. It has also been employed as a muniment room, as a Chapter-house, and (as now) as a practising room for the choir.

Near the south-western pier of the central tower access can

be obtained to what remains of the **Saxon Church.** It was when the foundations of this pier were reached, in 1887, that the first indications of an earlier building were brought to light. First a solid piece of wall was discovered, and soon after a substantial piece of cement attached to the wall, running north and south, which has since proved to be the eastern wall of the north transept of the Saxon Church. The workmen also came upon a plaster floor, on which were remains of burnt wood, reddened stone, and other evidences of a conflagration. As the work of excavation proceeded at intervals, fresh discoveries were made. The walls of the north transept, choir, and part of the south transept, can be traced. Just outside the eastern wall can be seen portions of two Saxon tombs which were originally in the grave-yard.

EVANGELISTIC SYMBOL FROM GROINED ROOF OF LANTERN TOWER. DRAWN BY W. H. LORD.

The width of both choir and transepts is about 23 feet. The choir was not apsidal. The south wall of the south transept was just beyond the wall of the existing building; the extreme east end was almost exactly underneath the pillars in the present transept; the west wall of the south transept of the Saxon church was under the practising room; the nave extended into the cloister court. Near the south end of the excavations was discovered a portion of a Saxon altar *in situ*. No remains have been found of the nave.

The roofs of both transepts are flat, and, except where rotten boards have been replaced, original. They are now uncoloured, but formerly were painted in black and white diamond patterns. All the windows at the north and south ends are Norman, with Perpendicular tracery.

The lantern tower has a fine groined roof, carefully restored and well painted. In the centre is a representation of the Saviour; eight coloured shields have the emblems of the Passion; four have the evangelistic symbols.

The Nave, notwithstanding the years it took to build, the change of architecture that was coming into use as it was being finished, and the alteration in plan that was decided upon towards the end, is a very complete and almost uniform structure. There are ten bays, all having round arches; in the triforium each large arch has two smaller ones beneath it; and in each bay of the clerestory is one high arch and two smaller ones. The triforium arches in the two easternmost

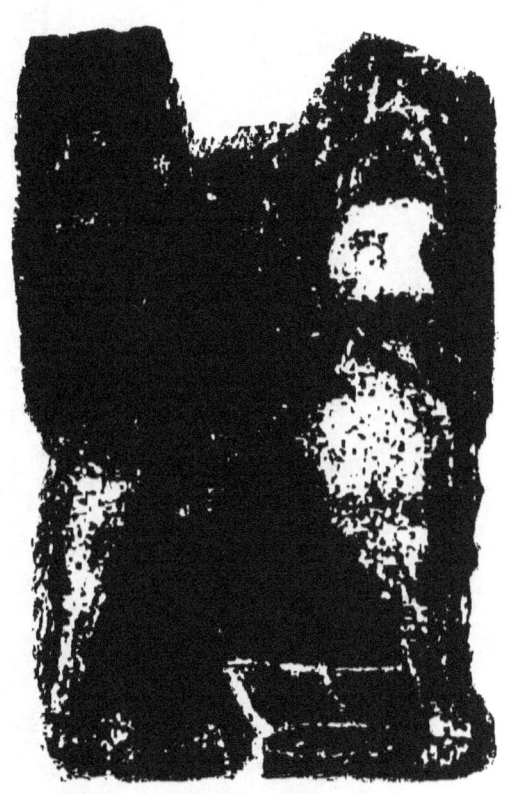

EVANGELISTIC SYMBOL FROM GROINED ROOF OF LANTERN TOWER. DRAWN BY W. H. LORD.

bays, on both sides, have the hatchet ornamentation in the tympanum; this may either mark the limits of the old Benedictine choir, or may simply suggest earlier work. Almost the only indication of distinct later work, as we proceed towards

WOODEN BOSS FROM GROINED ROOF OF LANTERN TOWER.
DRAWN BY W. H. LORD.

the west, is in the different forms of the bases of the piers. The arcading of the aisles curiously changes towards the west in both aisles, but not at corresponding points; the change consists in the reversing the interlacing of the arches. The third pillars from the west end on either side are not really, strictly speaking, pillars at all. They were built as supports to two western towers which it was intended certainly to erect at this point, even if they were not at least in part built. There are many other little details in the neighbourhood of these piers, all confirming Mr Paley's discovery with respect to these contemplated towers, one at any rate of which he thinks was actually erected. The pillars are cylindrical

hotochrom Co., Ld., Photo.]

THE NAVE, LOOKING EAST.

with numerous attached shafts. In addition to the changed form of the bases, careful observers can detect proofs of later work in the capitals of the shafts in the triforium. In front of each pier a shaft rises to the roof; and on these the original ceiling rested. On some of the piers in the south aisle, near the west end, may be seen several very curious masons' marks. In the nave is a very massive pulpit given in 1873 by the family of Dr James, for forty years Canon, bearing an inscription to his memory. It is from the design of Mr Edward

Barry, and was meant to be in keeping with the Norman architecture of the nave. The central shaft is of Devonshire marble, the main body of the pulpit of red Dumfries stone, and some of the smaller pillars are of green Greek marble. At the angles are four large figures of the Evangelists. There is also in the nave a wooden eagle lectern, carved by the late Rev. R. S. Baker, Rector of Hargrave.

The Nave Ceiling is very curious and remarkable. If originally flat, and supported on the tall shafts last mentioned, it would be just above the great arch of the central tower before that was altered from the round form. It is supposed that this was the case; and that when the pointed arch was substituted the central compartment of the ceiling was raised, and the two outer ones made to slope as we see it now. But if the Norman roof was flat, its outer compartments would manifestly not be broad enough to fill the space now occupied by the sloping sides. And yet there is no alteration in the style of ornamentation: nor are the diamonds, which are divided by the line where the slope joins the horizontal portion, unduly elongated, as would seem to be necessary in the part nearest the wall. Some change was clearly made when the Decorated arches were built; for above the Norman cornice on which the roof was originally laid, there is now a length of painted wood containing coats of arms obviously of later date than the ceiling. It is not possible to pronounce with certainty on the question. But considering (1), that the whole ceiling was certainly raised in consequence of the superior height of the tower arch (2), that no difference can be detected between the centre compartments and those at the side in the patterns, and (3), that additional height has been secured by the Decorated boarding above mentioned, the most probable solution seems to be that the whole is the original Norman work, practically unaltered, and that it was never flat, but had always sloping sides as at present. All agree that the style of the painting is perfectly characteristic of the period. The divisions are of the lozenge shape; in each lozenge of the central line is a figure, and in each alternate one of the sides. The middle set has more elongated lozenges than the others. The borders are black and white, with some coloured lines, in odd zigzag patterns. The figures, which are mostly seated, are very quaint and strange. Some are sacred, some grotesque.

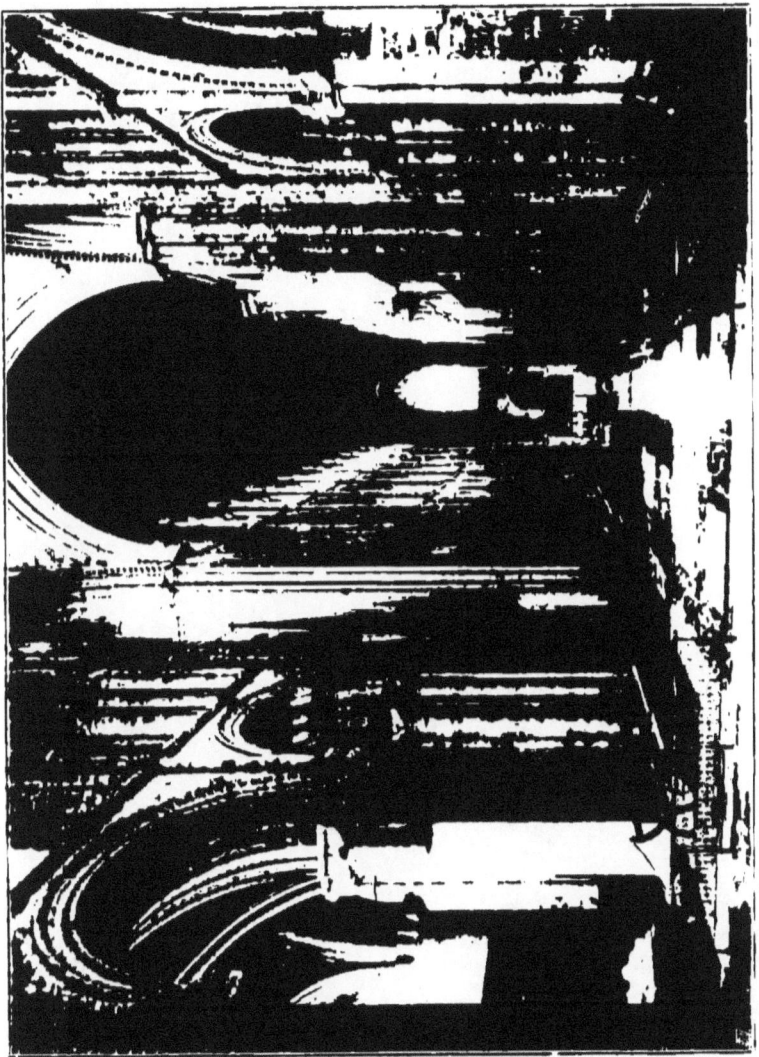

Photochrom Co., Ld., Photo THE CHOIR AND NAVE, LOOKING WEST.

We can see S. Peter with the keys, kings, queens, and minstrels; we find also a head with two faces, a monkey riding backwards on a goat, a human figure with head and hoofs of an ass, a horse playing a harp, a winged dragon, a dancing lion, an eagle, and other curious devices.

The West Transept extends beyond the aisles. The huge pointed arches covered with Norman mouldings are very remarkable. The arcading which goes round the lower part of the aisle walls was continued round the east sides and the ends of this transept, but it has all been hacked away, and the walls now are flat. This has been done within the present century; the position of the arcade is very plainly to be seen. The south end is used as a baptistery, which is railed off. The font is of a local marble of thirteenth century date; but the lower part is modern. For many years it was used as a flower pot in one of the prebendal gardens, whence it was removed by Dean Monk and ultimately restored to its original use. In the early part of the last century a font stood by the second pillar on the north side of the nave. This had been erected in 1615, as appears by an entry in the cathedral register of that date, when the son of one of the prebendaries was baptized "in the new font in the bodye of the Cathedral Church here." The north end of this transept is used as a vestry. It is screened off, with the adjacent bays of the north aisle, by some of the woodwork that has been removed from Dean Monk's choir. From these specimens the general character of the whole can be easily gathered.

The west wall has no trace of Norman work. The arcade by the ground consists of pointed arches, though the great doorway has a round arch; all have Early English mouldings. The great doors themselves are of the same date, as shown by the carved capital at the top. The east window, with its Perpendicular tracery, is set inside an Early English arch, which has two lofty lancets by the side; and in looking at it from the east it can hardly be detected that this arch is not the very framework of the window. The very lofty lancets on the east of the projecting parts of this transept, as well as the decoration of the arches in the triforium above the aisles, should be noticed.

The number of **Altars** in the church was considerable. They were of course all served by members of the foundation,

but they had not separate endowments like chantries in a
parish church. Nor does any one appear to have been
associated with any company or guild. There were, besides
the High Altar and that in the Lady Chapel, three in the new
building, one in the little chapel between the choir and Lady
Chapel, one in each choir aisle, two (SS. John and James)
in the north transept, four (SS. Oswald, Benedict, and Kyneburga, and the Holy Trinity) in the south transept, two (the
Ostrie Chapel and that of the Holy Spirit) in the building
west of the south transept, one in the rood-loft, most likely four
against pillars in the nave (a bracket on a pillar on the north
side marks the position of one), and apparently one in the
south part of the west transept. If this enumeration is correct
there were not less than twenty-two. There seems also to have
been an altar in the hearse over Queen Katherine's tomb;
and, though no mention of them occurs, we should suppose
there must have been one on each side of the entrance
beneath the rood-loft.

Two altar-stones only have been found. One is marked on
a plan made about 180 years ago as being laid down in the
choir a little to the east of where the eagle lectern now stands.
It was subsequently taken up, sawn into three pieces, and
placed beneath the arch leading from the western transept to
the south aisle. Some twenty-five years ago it was again
removed from the pavement and is preserved elsewhere. The
five crosses are large and deeply cut, and are in the form
of cross-crosslets. The other has been taken up from the
pavement quite recently. It is a very curious example, and
one that might well escape notice.[1] The stone is of the usual
size, and uninscribed. It is much worn by constant treadings,
and the five crosses are nearly obliterated, though quite distinctly to be seen. But instead of there being, as usual, one in
each corner of the stone, or nearly so, all the five are towards
the centre of the stone, within a space of about two square
feet.

Of Stained Glass the only ancient examples are some fragments that have been collected from different parts of the
church, mostly as it seems from the cloisters, and put together

---

[1] The present writer, who has copied every inscription in the church,
and examined (so he believed) every stone in the floor over and over
again, never found it out.

in two central windows in the apse. These are well worth observing with care. No scenes of course can be made out, but the faces, when examined closely, are found to be singularly good. Most of the pieces formed portions of a window or

HEAD OF S. PETER IN ANCIENT STAINED GLASS IN THE APSE.
DRAWN BY W. H. LORD.

series of windows representing incidents in the life of S. Peter. This is apparent from the few words that can still be made out on the labels, which are all fragments of texts referring to that

Saint. A few of the texts have been reversed. Among them are these: *Pasce oves; domine non erit; es Christus; non sapis ea que; Beatus es Simon Barjona; domine bonum est nos esse; super hanc pe; quia caro; quem esse dicitis.* These fragments were placed in their present position by Dean Tarrant. The modern glass is inconsiderable in quantity, and of no very conspicuous merit. Two in the new building are perhaps the best. One is to the memory of Dean Butler, "the offering of his widow"; the other was given by Canon Argles (afterwards Dean) in memory of his father-in-law, Bishop Davys, "Illustriss. Reginæ Victoriæ Preceptoris." This window takes the place of one which had been for many years an eyesore, being filled with blue, green, and yellow glass in a kaleidoscope pattern. But when first put in, a hundred years ago, it was much admired. An account of it at the time calls it "a beautiful window of stained glass in various colours, and formed by the late Thomas Cooper, an ingenious workman." In the north choir aisle is a memorial window to Thomas Mills, Hon. Canon, 1856. In the south transept some in memory of Payne Edwards, LL.B., 1861; Sir Chapman Marshall, Kt., Alderman of London, whose son was Precentor here; and James Cattel, cathedral librarian, 1877. In the north transept are several given by Mr G. W. Johnson, two in memory of his father and mother, one to the Prince Consort, and some unconnected with any names; there are also two in memory of George John Gates, 1860, and John Hewitt Paley "juvenis desideratissimi," 1857.

The architecture of **The Parvise**, over the western porch, has been already described. It now contains the library, removed to this place from the new building by Dean Tarrant. The collection was begun by Dean Duport, who presented books himself, and obtained more from the Prebendaries and other persons; it was afterwards enriched with the whole of the valuable library of Bishop Kennett, and part of Dean Lockier's, and has since had many considerable additions. The manuscripts are not numerous, the chief being the very important book known as Swapham. The greater part of this has been printed by Sparkes. His publication includes Abbot John's Chronicle, The History of Burgh by Hugo Candidus with its continuation by Swapham, the Chronicle of Walter of Whittlesey, and two other works. There are also kept here some of the fabric rolls of the monastery. Bishop Kennett's library contained a most valuable collection of tracts and pamphlets published in the latter part of the seventeenth century. There are also some books of much earlier date, a few of great rarity. A memorandum written in the Book of Swapham above mentioned tells us that the Precentor, Humphrey Austin, had hidden it in 1642 in anticipation of coming troubles. But Cromwell's soldiers found it, and would probably have destroyed it; the Precentor, however, under pretence of enquiring after an old Latin bible, found out where it was, and redeemed it for the sum of ten shillings.

Monuments and Inscriptions.—We proceed to speak of these, treated as a single subject, instead of describing them at the various parts of the building where they are to be found.

At first sight it is thought that this cathedral is singularly deficient in monuments of interest. To a certain extent this is the case. There are no memorial chantries, such as add to the beauty of many of our noblest churches; no effigies of warriors or statesmen; no series of ancient tablets or inscriptions that illustrate the history of the neighbourhood; not a single brass. With few exceptions all the monuments and inscriptions that remain commemorate abbots or other members of the monastery, or, after the Reformation, bishops, and members of the cathedral foundation and their families. While of famous persons known to have been buried within the walls, such as Katherine of Arragon, Mary Queen of Scots, the Archbishops Elfricus and Kinsius of York, Sir Geoffrey de la Mare, Sir Robert de Thorpe, and others, no memorials worthy of their fame and importance are in existence. The wanton destruction during the civil war in great part explains this; but it is sad to remember that numbers of mediæval inscriptions in the floor were hidden or destroyed during some well-meaning but ill-judged alterations in the last century.

First in interest and importance is that known as the Monks' Stone, now preserved in the new building. It is generally thought that this was constructed in commemoration of the massacre of Abbot Hedda and his monks in 870, by the Danes. It was not till nearly a century later that any attempt was made to rebuild the monastery. But Mr Bloxam read a paper at Peterborough in 1861 in which he disputed the authenticity of this monument, which had been previously regarded as one of the most ancient monumental stones extant. He pronounced it to be Norman, and not Saxon work, and some centuries later in date than the massacre of the monks. He considered the figures did not represent the slain monks and their abbot, but Christ and eleven disciples. It has been further conjectured by Bishop Westcott that it may have been part of the shrine erected over the relics of S. Kyneburga, when they were removed from Castor to Peterborough in the former half of the eleventh century. A fragment of sculpture in the same style is built into the west wall of the south transept. Even if the latter years of the ninth century are deemed too early a date for the stone, at any rate the style of the sculpture and ornamentation seems much earlier than anything we can now see in position in the building itself. May it not have been erected when the minster was reconstructed at the end of the tenth century? It was formerly in the churchyard; sometimes testators (like Dr Pocklington) desired in their wills that they might be interred near it. It has been usually stated that the stone was erected by Abbot Godric of Crowland, who died in 941. Unvarying tradition has associated it with the Danish massacre; its dimensions almost exactly agree with the earliest records of the stone said to have been so erected. The cruciform nimbus round the head of one figure leaves no doubt that it was designed for the Saviour; but this had been recognised many years before Mr Bloxam wrote.

PART OF THE MONKS' STONE.
DRAWN BY W. H. LORD.

In the north transept, below the level of the floor, and protected by wooden doors, are several richly ornamented slabs or coffin lids, of undoubted Saxon date; and they form a series which may be considered one of the very best in England. They are in their original position, the spot on which they lie being outside the Saxon church, and they were then in the grave-yard. They were discovered in 1888. The interlacing work, and other carvings, are deeply cut and in excellent preservation.

The six recumbent effigies of abbots are the very best series of Benedictine memorials in the country. Attempts have been made to identify them from the character of the carvings. But as four are certainly of thirteenth century date, and one late in the twelfth century, and as thirteen abbots ruled during that period, it may be pronounced impossible to name each one. One only, manifestly the latest in date, and also in poorest preservation (being carved in clunch), has the mitre; this is now temporarily placed in the new building; there is little doubt that it represents John Chambers, the last Abbot and first Bishop. All the other five abbots are represented in alb and chasuble, holding a book (signifying, it is said, the statutes of the Benedictine order), in the left hand; while in the right hand is a crosier. In one instance this is not very clear. Four have their feet resting on fanciful creatures, which, in three cases, hold the lower ends of the crosiers in their mouths. Two of these crosiers, at least, are turned outwards: this is contrary to the commonly received opinion that the turning inward symbolised the domestic rule over a monastic house. The head of one abbot rests on a square cushion. Four of these effigies are in the south choir aisle; one of them being beneath the Norman sepulchral arch raised to commemorate three abbots, John de Sais, who died in 1125, Martin of Bec, in 1155, and Andrew, in 1199. It seems unlikely that the one placed beneath the

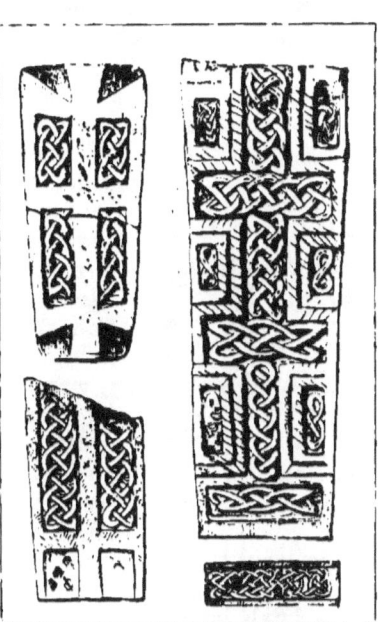

SAXON COFFIN LIDS IN NORTH TRANSEPT. DRAWN BY W. H. LORD.

arch should represent one of those three, although usually assigned to the latest, Andrew. The next two in the aisle were found in the ruins of the old chapter-house, and brought into the church.[1] The date of the easternmost is known. It is more richly ornamented than the rest, and the entire coffin is above ground, with handsome quatrefoils and other carving. This commemorates Alexander of Holderness, 1226. It was found under the woodwork of the old choir which was removed in 1830, beneath the second arch, on the north of the choir. The coffin contained the body, in a large coarse garment, with boots on, and a crosier in the left hand. The boots were what are called "rights and lefts," and in fair preservation. The head was gone. A piece of lead was found inscribed "Abbas : Alexandr : " The remains were gathered together and re-interred beneath the present position of the coffin. At the same time in all likelihood the effigy that was already on the spot (one of those that had been found in the ruins of the chapter-house) was removed to one of the chapels in the south transept ; from which place it was afterwards moved to the new building immediately behind the apse, where now is the monument to Bishop Chambers ; and now it has been put on a stone plinth on the spot where the coffin of Abbot Alexander was found, under the mistaken impression that it was the figure found there in 1830.

PORTION OF A MONUMENT OF AN ABBOT.

The other præ-Reformation memorials are very few. Two have lately been found concealed by the paving, Abbot Godfrey, 1321, moved from the choir to the north aisle, and sub-prior Fraunceys, at the east end of the south nave aisle. In the morning chapel is an early stone with inscription in capitals, and three stone coffin lids ; other fragmentary inscriptions remain in S. Oswald's chapel, in the north choir aisle, and under the bell-tower.

In the floor on the north side of the choir, near the altar rails, is a stone with modern inscription recording the burial

---

[1] As well as one other, probably the one now under one of the arches on the north of the choir.

places of Elfricus and Kinsius, both Archbishops of York; the former died in 1051, the latter in 1060. An old guide-book says that "on the north side, in two hollow places of wall, were found two chests about three feet long, in each of which were the bones of a man: and of whom appeared by a plate of lead in each chest, whereon the name of the person was engraved," these names being those given above. The chronicle expressly records of Kinsius, "*jacet tumulatus in scrinio juxta magnum altare in parte boreali.*"

TOMB OF AN ABBOT IN NORTH CHOIR AISLE. DRAWN BY W. H. LORD.

Queen Katherine of Arragon was buried in the north choir aisle, just outside the most eastern arch, in 1535. A hearse was placed near, probably between the two piers. Four years later this is described as "the inclosed place where the Lady Katherine lieth," and there seems to have been a small altar within it. Some banners that adorned it remained in the cathedral till 1586. About the same time some persons were imprisoned for defacing the "monument," and required to "reform the same." The only monument, strictly so called, of which there is any record, was a low table monument, raised on two shallow steps, with simple quatrefoils, carved in squares set diamond-wise. Engravings of this shew it to have been an insignificant and mean erection. A few slabs of it were lately found buried beneath the floor, and they are now placed against the wall of the aisle. One of the prebendaries repaired this monument at his own cost, about 1725, and supplied a tiny brass plate with name and date, part of which remains in the floor. This monument was removed in 1792. A handsome marble stone has quite recently been laid down to the Queen's memory above her grave, with incised inscription and coats of arms.

A tablet has been erected in the south choir aisle to record the fact that Mary Queen of Scots had been buried near the spot. Recent explorations have proved that the exact spot was just within the choir. The funeral took place on the first of August, 1587. Remains of the hearse between the pillars were to be seen so lately as 1800. On Oct. 11, 1612, the body was removed to Westminster Abbey, by order of King James I., the Queen's son. A photograph of the letter ordering the removal, the original of which is still in possession of the Dean and Chapter, is framed and hung on an adjacent pillar.

PORTION OF MONUMENT OF AN ABBOT.

In the south choir aisle is a fine monument with a life-size effigy of Archbishop Magee in his robes. It is carved in pure white marble. On the side are impaled coats of arms and an inscription. The likeness is excellent.

The other tablets and inscriptions hardly require detailed descriptions. In the new building is the mutilated monument to Sir Humfrey Orme: no names or dates remain; at the top are the words *Sangvis Iesv Christi pvrgat nos ab omnibvs Peccatis nostris.* Near this is an elaborate erection to Thomas Deacon, 1721, a great benefactor to the town. On a stone to John Brimble, organist of S. John's College, Cambridge, 1670, we read that he was *Musis et musicæ devotissimus, ad cælestem evectus Academiam.* Among many inscriptions some interesting items will be found. John Benson, 1827, was the "oldest Committee Clerk at the House of Commons." Humfrey Orme, 1670, was *A supremo Angliæ senatu ad superiorem sanctorum conventum evocatus.* On the memorial to Bishop Madan, 1813, are the lines :—

TOMB OF AN ABBOT IN SOUTH CHOIR AISLE. DRAWN BY W. H. LORD.

In sacred sleep the pious Bishop lies,
Say not in death—A good Man never dies.

On the tablet to Bishop Cumberland, 1718, are four Latin

lines from Dean Duport's epigram upon the Bishop's confutation of Hobbes. In the south choir aisle, on the tablet to Dean Lockier, 1740, is the only instance of the arms of the Deanery

Photochrom Co., Ld., Photo.]
SOUTH AISLES OF CHOIR AND NAVE.

impaling another shield, on a monument. Near this is a wooden tablet executed in good taste, recording the fact that the iron screens are a memorial to Dean Argles, whose munificent contributions to the embellishment of the cathedral are well known. The Norman arch at the west end of this aisle has a modern painted inscription, believed to be an exact copy of the original :—

> *Hos tres Abbates, Quibus est Prior Abba Johannes*
> *Alter Martinus, Andreas Ultimus, unus*
> *Hic claudit Tumulus ; pro Clausis ergo rogemus.*

Near this is a tablet to Roger Pemberton, 1695, with a line from Homer in Greek at the top, thus rendered in Lord Derby's translation, "The race of men is as the race of leaves." In the north choir aisle John Workman, Prebendary, 1685, is described as *Proto-Canonicus*, probably meaning that he held the first stall. The tablet to Frances Cosin, wife of the Dean afterwards Bishop of Durham, was not erected till after the Bishop's death in 1672, though she died in 1642. The Bishop left £40 by his will for this monument, and prescribed the words of the inscription. On the very large tablet above the piscina is a punning motto, *Temperantia te Temperatrice*, the person commemorated being Richard Tryce, 1767.

Last of all we must speak of the one memorial which is usually looked at first, the famous picture of Old Scarlett, on the wall of the western transept. He is represented with a spade, pickaxe, keys, and a whip in his leathern girdle ; at his feet is a skull. At the top of the picture are the arms of the cathedral. Beneath the portrait are these lines :—

> YOV SEE OLD SCARLEITS PICTVRE STAND ON HIE
> BVT AT YOVR FEETE THERE DOTH HIS BODY LYE
> HIS GRAVESTONE DOTH HIS AGE AND DEATH TIME SHOW
> HIS OFFICE BY THEIS TOKENS YOV MAY KNOW
> SECOND TO NONE FOR STRENGTH AND STVRDYE LIMM
> A SCARBABE MIGHTY VOICE WITH VISAGE GRIM
> HEE HAD INTER'D TWO QVEENES WITHIN THIS PLACE
> AND THIS TOWNES HOVSEHOLDERS IN HIS LIVES SPACE
> TWICE OVER : BVT AT LENGTH HIS ONE TVRNE CAME
> WHAT HEE FOR OTHERS DID FOR HIM THE SAME
> WAS DONE : NO DOVBT HIS SOVL DOTH LIVE FOR AYE
> IN HEAVEN : THOVGH HERE HIS BODY CLAD IN CLAY.

On the floor is a stone inscribed : "Ivly 2 1594 R S ætatis 98." This painting is not a contemporary portrait, but a copy made in 1747. In 1866 it was sent on loan to the South Kensington Museum.

PETERBOROUGH—SOUTH SIDE OF CLOSE IN 1801.

CHAPTER IV.

THE MINSTER PRECINCTS AND CITY.

THERE are many objects of great interest to be seen in the Minster Yard. This name is not unfrequently given to the whole of the territory belonging to the Dean and Chapter surrounding the church. The correct title is, however, as given above, the Minster Precincts; and it is by this name that the parish is described, for the Abbey Church, like a few others, is a parish church, as well as the Cathedral of the diocese. Although without churchwardens, this parish still appoints its own overseers of the poor. Old residents distinguish the Close from the Precincts, limiting the use of the former expression to the area west of the Cathedral. Contrary to what all would expect, the great gateway to the west is not the boundary of the Precincts, for they extend a little further west, and include one or two houses beyond the gateway.

This ancient entrance to the monastic grounds naturally first arrests the attention. It was built by Abbot Benedict in the last quarter of the twelfth century. Though it has been much altered, a considerable part of the original structure remains. As we see it from the Market-place we observe a fifteenth century look about it: on closer inspection we see that a Perpendicular arch has been built in front of the Norman arch, and that a facing of the same date has been carried above. Here is an arcade, with the alternate panels pierced for windows. On each side of the gateway are also good Norman arcades; the doorway in the arcade to the north opens into a residence, that on the south gives access to the room above. This was originally the Chapel of S. Nicolas. On the eastern side of the room is a three-light window, manifestly a late insertion, and adapted from some other building. It is said to be part of a shrine which formerly was in the Cathedral, a portion of which still remains in the new building. This statement has been repeated over and over again; but it is difficult to see any resemblance between the two.

The chapel over the gateway has been put to various uses since the dissolution of monasteries. In 1617 it was assigned to the porter as part of his residence. At a later period it was let. It has served the purposes of a muniment room, a Masonic lodge room, a tailor's workshop, a practising room for the choristers, a class-room for the Grammar School. In the flourishing days of the Gentlemen's Society, when members met and read papers, and kept up a considerable literary correspondence with learned men in various parts of the kingdom, its meetings were held here; and it is now used as the library of the same society, which was founded here in 1730 as a branch of the Spalding Society "for the promotion of friendship and literature," though it is understood now to be nothing more than a circulating library. There are some valuable books in the collection.

On the left hand, as we pass through the gate, is all that remains of the **Chapel of S. Thomas of Canterbury.** It is the chancel of a much larger building. Originally the chapel was begun by Waterville and finished by Benedict: it was therefore of Norman date. The present chancel was built in the latter part of the fourteenth century. While the east window, with its graceful net tracery and very elegant cross above, might suggest an earlier date, yet a glance at the side windows, which are distinctly of transitional character, tells us that 1360 or 1370 may be assigned as the period of erection. About 1404 the abbey gave the materials of the nave of this chapel to the town, to assist in rebuilding the parish church on the present site; but the chancel had been too recently built to be removed. Since the establishment of the Cathedral the chancel seems always to have been used as the Cathedral Grammar School, until the year 1885, when the School was removed to new buildings in the Park Road. It now contains the collections of the Natural History and Archæological Society.

THE MINSTER PRECINCTS AND CITY.

All the other ancient buildings on the west, the Plumber's Office, the Sister House, the Treasurer's Office, have long disappeared. The Minster Almshouses, adjoining the wall of the Deanery garden, are the only buildings on the north side. They have no ancient features.

The door immediately to the right of the great gateway as we enter the close leads to a vaulted chamber which was once the gaol. A few steps bring us to a very magnificent gateway, leading to the Palace grounds, over which is a chamber, called the **Knights' Chamber.** This is of Early English date, with a fine groined roof. The gates and postern are placed at some distance from the outer archway, adding greatly to the dignity and effect of the whole composition. The delicate arcading of the sides, and the excellent clustered shafts, are good examples of the period: unfortunately the bases of the shafts are now hidden by accumulation of earth. On the north and south faces are long niches with figures: three on the north are said to be King Edward II., and the Abbot and Prior of the period; those on the south are Apostles. The chamber above is used as a muniment room.

GATEWAY TO THE CATHEDRAL IN 1791.

Much of the line of buildings to the east of this gateway is modern, but it harmonises excellently with the ancient work. Near the Cathedral is some mediæval work, and the office at the end, on the ground floor, has a good stone groined roof. This is believed to have been the Penitentiary.

The **Deanery Gateway**, at the north-eastern corner of the close is a fine specimen of architecture. In the spandrels above the great four-centred arch are two coats of arms, one with the keys and crosslets, the other with swords and crosses. These are now the arms of the See and the Cathedral respectively: but it is difficult to say what was their special significance when this gate was erected. Are we to suppose that the Abbot and Prior used different armorial bearings before the Reformation? Above the smaller door is a boldly carved rebus of the Abbot in whose time the gate was erected, a church on a tun, Robert Kirton (Kirkton). His initials in stone are also carved beneath the parapet. Several of the details are well worthy of attention. We find the Tudor rose and portcullis; the arms of S. Edward and of S. Edmund, the Martyr King; an early instance in stone of the Prince of Wales' feathers; and the triangular symbol of the Holy Trinity. The date is about 1520.

Through an open archway to the east we enter the burial ground. Until 1804 this was the only place of burial for the whole city. On the left is the Deanery, but nothing of antiquity is to be seen from the exterior. In the hall are some good fragments of old glass, some of it probably part of the original embellishments of the house, though some may have been brought from the Cathedral, and some is again quite modern. Some panels of early date, brought from another room, have also lately been put up in the hall. The churchyard has been planted with trees and shrubs, and is well kept. It has, however, become much more publicly used within the last twenty-five or thirty years, owing to a thoroughfare for foot-passengers which has been opened at the north-western end of the close; and the usual results of such publicity have followed in the treading down of the turf and in the damage inflicted on the shrubs. One of the most striking views of the Cathedral is seen from the north-eastern corner of the precincts, near the house known as "The Vineyard." This was the house occupied by the officers who came down to superintend the spoliation of the building in 1643. This view takes in the whole of the great length of the Cathedral, the bell-tower and the north-western spire forming a very effective group.

Passing round the east end and proceeding to the south we come to the ruins of the **Infirmary.** Here we may see some very excellent Early English work, most elegant and graceful. It was erected about 1260. The plan was similar to a large church with aisles. The nave was used as the hall, the aisles were the quarters of the inmates, and the chancel was the chapel of the institution. Many of the main arches remain, and the details of the ornamentation and mouldings will repay careful study. At the west end is a very perfect piece of arcading. The large arch, seen above a low wall to the east, was the arch leading to the chapel; in exactly the same position as the chancel arch in a church. At each side of this arch is a lancet never pierced. The main arch is now blocked up, forming a wall to one of the prebendal houses. The dining room of this same house was the Infirmarer's house, and has much very interesting Early English work. To the south of the Infirmary is another ancient house, though much modernised. This has always been a residence, and is now assigned to the Archdeacon of Northampton. Before entering the Cloister court we pass through the old slype, once a simple vaulted passage, but now open to the sky. It was the means of communication between the Refectory, which was situated to the west, and the Chapter House, which was on the east side of the Cloister. Quite recently one of the arches on the west side has been opened to view.

The **Cloister Court** is always called the Laurel Court. The origin of this name is not known. The northern part of the area covers the site of the nave of the Saxon church; but though search was made, during the recent works, for remains of the old foundations, nothing was discovered. On the south and west sides are to be seen remains of the arches and groining, but the appearance of the south wall of the cathedral suggests that there could not have been any covered alley to the north, so completely have all evidences of such an erection been removed. But it is known that there did exist an alley there, when the Cloisters were complete; for Gunton, describing it, says "The Cloyster about four square, in length 168 yards, in breadth 6 yards." The windows, contrary to the usual practice, were all glazed, and they contained a very fine series of painted glass, all destroyed in 1643. Gunton gives the subjects:—"The windows were all compleat and fair, adorned with glass of excellent painting : In the South Cloyster was the History of the Old Testament : In the East Cloyster of the New : In the North Cloyster, the Figures of the successive Kings from King Peada : In the West Cloyster, was the History from the foundation of the Monastery of King Peada, to the restoring of it by King Edgar." Each light had two lines of verse at the foot, explaining the subject matter of the

DOOR TO PALACE GROUNDS FROM THE CLOISTER IN 1797.

glass above. All the verses in the windows of the west alley are given; and from this we gather that there were nine windows there of four lights each. Although Gunton only gives the verses belonging to the west cloister, yet as he said previously that "every window had at the bottom the explanation of the history thus in verse," it is supposed that similar legends appeared in all the other alleys of the cloister. The verses are very quaint.

The archway at the south-eastern corner is very elegant, the open quatrefoil above the round arch and below the pointed

DOOR-WAY TO CATHEDRAL FROM CLOISTER COURT, NORTH-EAST.
DRAWN BY H. P. CLIFFORD.

arch being especially good. The south wall indicates that there were two sets of cloisters here, as the remains of early

English arcading are to be clearly seen. Towards the west was the lavatory, the remains indicating work of late fourteenth century date. It is on record that Robert of Lindsey (1214–1222) erected a lavatory in the south cloister: this would be contemporary with the Early English work remaining in this wall, and with the archway to the slype; but it must have been removed when the cloisters were enlarged, and another lavatory, of which we see the remains under three arches, built in its stead. The Refectory was immediately to the south of this wall: some beautiful carving is to be seen in the Bishop's garden. The south-western doorway gives access to the Bishop's grounds. The depth of the hollows behind the carved foliage above the door is remarkable.

In the west wall are remains of a Norman cloister; there are three arches and a door. From the architectural character it seems almost certain that these are older than any part of the present Cathedral. William of Waterville (1155–1175) "built the Cloister and covered it with lead." Canon Davys conjectures that this Abbot in reality repaired and made sound the old cloisters that had been built by Ernulf (1107–1115), "whose recent additions to the buildings of the monastery, we learn, alone escaped the fire, which consumed the other parts of the Abbey in the time of John de Sais." One of these arches has the cheese moulding; and on each jamb is a small incised cross, a very few inches long. If these are consecration crosses they are the only ones that have been noticed in any part of the Abbey.

On the west wall of the south transept aisle can be seen some stone brackets. These shew that after the destruction of the ancient cloister a covered way of some kind was erected here. Marks can also be seen, in the masonry, which indicate that originally this aisle had three gables. Two of the Norman buttresses of the south nave aisle have very curious terminations, which might well puzzle any observer. They are fireplaces for the use of plumbers. Passing through the Norman doorway at the north-western corner of the Laurel Court, we come into a narrow passage leading to the Minster Close.

In the **Bishop's Palace**, besides the remains of the Refectory, which, though so scanty, shew what a beautiful building it once was, there is very little worthy of note. The hall is a vaulted chamber, of no great height, with piers to support the

ARCHWAY FROM CLOISTER COURT, NORTH-WEST.
DRAWN BY H. P. CLIFFORD.

roof; most of it is part of the Abbot's dwelling, and of thirteenth century date. The Heaven's Gate Chamber, previously noticed, built by Abbot Kirton (1496-1528), lies to the south-east of the hall. The chapel was erected by Bishop Magee soon after he came to the diocese.

The City.—The mother church of S. John the Baptist is the only parish church in the city of mediæval date. Until 1856 it was the only parish church in the place. Originally the church stood east of the Minster. But, following what seems to be almost a universal law, the main population spread westward as the number of inhabitants increased, and the earlier buildings were left to the occupation of the poorer class. An insignificant little house in the old town is traditionally said to have been the Vicar's residence. It has some evidence of antiquity about it. The present church was built early in the fifteenth century. It was opened in 1407 with much solemnity by Abbot Genge. It is a spacious and dignified building, having a nave of seven bays; and there are two bays to the chancel, besides the sanctuary. The west tower is good, but hardly of sufficient dignity for such a church. The interior was reseated, and new roofs added, about fifteen years ago; they were designed by Mr Pearson. Much has been since done in the way of improving the interior by the addition of numerous stained glass windows. The great defect is the absence of screen-work: with a handsome chancel screen, and another to mark off the morning-service chapel in the south aisle, and with parcloses north and south of the chancel, this would be a grand church. There is at present an appearance of emptiness, notwithstanding the excellence of the modern wood-work. In 1891 the south porch was restored to the memory of Dr James (author of the well-known "Comment on the Collects," and many other theological works), formerly Vicar here. In the vestry, at the west end of the south aisle, is a large picture of King Charles I. Two curious specimens of early embroidery are here to be seen. They were once portions of altar-cloths, or of copes. In each case the work is in the form of a cross, about two feet long. Each has the figure of the Saviour on the Cross; but the details are not identical.

The Guild Hall, in the Market Place, is an effective little building, dated 1671. The lower part is open, and is used for the butter market. While sufficient for the transaction of

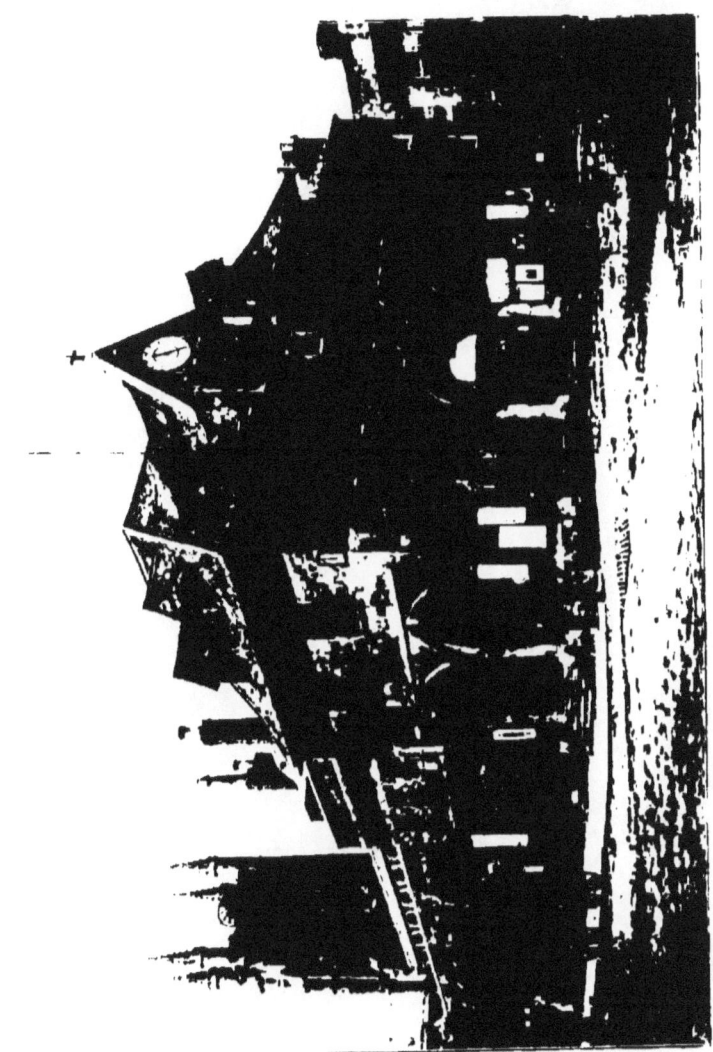

Photochrom Co., Ld., Photo.]

CHURCH OF S. JOHN THE BAPTIST AND GUILDHALL.

borough business 100 years ago, it is altogether inadequate now to the requirements of a corporation.

Until a very few years ago there was a mediæval building at Peterborough of the greatest interest. This was the old **Tithe Barn** of the Abbey, situated in the Manor of Boroughbury, on the Lincoln Road. It was much the finest in the kingdom. Unhappily the "enterprising builder" has obtained possession of it, and it has been pulled down, the materials, all Barnack stone, having been employed in building houses. It was of good thirteenth century work, and in perfect condition. On the east side were two large porches, by which a waggon fully laden could enter the barn. The roof was supported by very massive timbers rising from the ground, the whole arrangement resembling a wooden church with aisles. These timbers are indeed still standing: and the visitor interested in such edifices should not fail to inspect them.

CHAPTER V.

HISTORY OF THE MONASTERY.

THE inhabitants of the Fen country, when first distinguished by a special name, were known as the Gyrvii. Their district included the south part of Lincolnshire, the north part of Northamptonshire, and the greater part of Cambridgeshire. The southern Gyrvii were a province of East Anglia; the Gyrvii of the north appear to have been allied to the East Anglians, and perhaps inclined to become united with them; but they were ultimately absorbed in the great Midland Kingdom of Mercia. Bishop Stubbs,[1] speaking of the early Fasti of Peterborough, says: "Mercia, late in its formation as a kingdom, sprang at once into a great state under Penda: late in its adoption of Christianity, it seems from the period of its conversion to have taken a prominent place at once among the Christian powers. The Chronicle places the conversion in 655, and a very few years saw it the best governed and best organised province of the Church. In less than thirty years it was divided into five dioceses, amongst which the place of the Fen country is more clearly definable. The bishopric of Lindsey occupied the north of Lincolnshire, reaching to the Witham: a line drawn from the south point of Nottinghamshire to the Cam would probably represent the western border of the Gyrvii; the border of Cambridgeshire was the boundary of the dioceses of Elmham and Dunwich. The Fen country thus falls into the eastern portion of the great Lichfield diocese, which for a few years after 680 had its own bishop at Leicester, but was not finally separated from the mother see until 737."

[1] Archæological Journal, 1861, p. 196.

The date given above for the conversion of Mercia, 655, is the date of the laying of the foundation of the monastery of Medeshamstede. Penda had been succeeded on the throne of Mercia by his eldest son, Peada; and he, in conjunction with Oswy, brother of King Oswald, determined to "rear a minster to the glory of Christ and honour of Saint Peter."

Saxulf (656–675), was the first Abbot. In Bede no mention is made of royal patronage, and the whole credit of founding the abbey is given to Saxulf. Another account represents him as having been a thane of great wealth and renown, and that this abbey was dedicated by him "as the first fruits of the Mercian church." He was made Bishop of Lichfield in 675, but continued to take an active part in the affairs of the abbey. He died in 691.

Cuthbald (675), is named in the Chronicle as having been second Abbot. One of this name, possibly the same, was ruling the monastery at Oundle in 709, when S. Wilfrid died there. Nothing further is known of him; and nothing at all of **Egbald**, who appears in the usual lists as his successor.

The chroniclers give for the fourth Abbot one Pusa. But Bishop Stubbs has proved that **Bothwin** was Abbot from 758 to 789; and concludes that the introduction of Pusa into the list is a mistake, if not a mere invention.

Abbot **Beonna** came next, probably in 789 or very soon afterwards. "Possibly this Beonna is the same who was made Bishop of Hereford in 823, and died in 830."

Ceolred succeeded, and in the year 852 signs a grant of land as Abbot. Patrick conjectures that he became a bishop, but does not name his diocese. There is no certainty about the dates at which these early abbots entered upon their office; and possibly some names have been altogether lost. But all accounts agree that the last Abbot of Medeshamstede was **Hedda**; and that he perished when the monastery was destroyed and its inmates killed by the Danes in 870. A graphic account of the circumstances attending this attack is given by Ingulf; but as authentic historians like Orderic and Malmesbury have no reference whatever to the occurrences described by Ingulf, Bishop Stubbs unwillingly is obliged to consider his version to be a pure romance. But of the fact itself, the utter destruction of the monastery, there is no question; nor of the fact that all the inmates, or nearly all, perished. We read that at Crowland some monks escaped the general slaughter, and met again, after the departure of the Danes, and elected a fresh abbot. They then came to Medeshamstede, and buried the bodies of those that had been murdered, in one vast tomb. It has been commonly supposed that the Monks' Stone, before described, was the stone erected at the time in commemoration of the disaster. The arguments against this supposition have been already given.

The Fen monasteries remained desolate for 100 years. During that period the lands were constantly being seized by different intruders. It was not till the time of Alfred the Great, who came to the throne in 871, that the invasions of the Danes were finally checked, and tranquillity restored to the kingdom. Security being assured, the people began again to improve their public buildings and the religious houses. Crowland was the first in the neighbourhood to be restored. This restoration was effected by Thurketyl. Instigated probably by his example, Ethelwold, Bishop of Winchester, encouraged and supported by King Edgar, rebuilt the monastery of Medeshamstede after the old model. The rebuilding was completed in 972; and the name of Burgh was given to the place, and the old name went altogether out of use.

The first Abbot, after the re-establishment of the monastery, was **Aldulf** (971–992), formerly Chancellor to the King. He is said to have accidentally caused the death of his only son, and feeling that he could no longer live happily in the midst of earthly vanities, he endowed this monastery with all his possessions, and was appointed to govern it. Gunton declares that the prosperous and wealthy condition of the abbey under the rule of Aldulf caused its name to be improved into Gildenburgh, the Golden Borough. At this time most of the neighbouring woods were cut down and the land brought into cultivation. Aldulf became Bishop of Worcester after remaining twenty years at Burgh; and in 995 was made Archbishop of York. He died in May 1002, and is buried at Worcester. He held indeed the See of Worcester with that of York till his death.

He was succeeded at Burgh by **Kenulf** (992–1005). He

is described as famous for his wisdom and learning, and as having governed his abbey "most admirably and sweetly." In 1005 he was made Bishop of Winchester, not without suspicion of a corrupt purchase (*episcopatum nummis nundinatus fuerat*), and died the following year.

The next Abbot, **Elsinus** (1006–1055), was remarkable chiefly for the number of relics he collected, designing thereby to increase the fame and wealth of the monastery. Dean Patrick thinks that before Elsinus there was an abbot named KINSINUS, whose name he found in one record; but he adds that if he were really abbot it could at most have been for a few days or months. The list of relics gathered together by Elsinus is extensive. At least eighty are enumerated. It speaks volumes for the credulity of the age when we find in this list such things as the following :—A portion of Aaron's rod that budded; a portion of one of the five loaves that fed the five thousand; a shoulder-blade of one of the Holy Innocents; two pieces of the Virgin Mary's veil; part of the stone paten of the Evangelist S. John. The great relic of the house was the arm of S. Oswald. The date when this was acquired is not certainly known, some thinking that this period is too early a date to assign to its acquisition. Bede relates[1] "that this Oswald, King of Northumberland, was very free and liberal in giving of alms to the poor; and one day whilst he sate at meat, one of his servants told him of a great number of poor people come to his gate for relief; whereupon King Oswald sent them meat from his own table, and there not being enough to serve them all, he caused one of his silver dishes to be cut in pieces, and to be distributed amongst the rest; which Aydanus, a Bishop (who came out of Scotland to convert, and instruct those Northern parts of England), beholding, took the King by the right hand, saying, *nunquam inveterascat haec manus*, let this hand never wax old, or be corrupted; which came to pass. This arm was first deposited at Bamburgh, a religious place in Yorkshire. Walter of Whittlesey writing the story thereof, tells that it was brought to the monastery of Burgh by Winegotus of Bebeberch, but saith not when, therefore I cannot conjecture better than that it was by the procurement of this Abbot Elsinus. It is said that this arm wrought many cures upon several diseased folk; and that it was of such fame

---

[1] Gunton, p. 12; translated from Bede's Eccl. Hist. iii. 6.

in the days of King Stephen, as that he himself came to Peterburgh purposely to see it; and offered his ring to S. Oswald, and also remitted to the monastery the sum of forty marks wherein it was indebted unto him." It is specially recorded in the Chronicle that this abbot took advantage of the poverty of an abbey in Normandy, the district having been afflicted with a grievous famine, and purchased from it the body of S. Florentinus, with the exception of the head, for one hundred pounds of silver.

He was succeeded by **Arwinus** (1055-1057), a monk of the house, but he resigned the government in two years. Next came **Leofric** (1057-1066), a very eminent man, said to have been of royal descent. He was nephew to Leofric, Earl of Coventry. In the time of this abbot, William of Normandy invaded England, and Leofric was for some time with the English army. But in consequence of ill health he was obliged to leave it and return to his monastery, where he died the same year. He is highly praised in the Chronicle as "*pulcherrimus Monachorum, flos et decus Abbatum.*"

Brando (1066-1069), succeeded, and greatly offended King William by applying to Edgar Atheling for confirmation of his appointment. He was uncle to Hereward, the Saxon patriot, and created him knight. At his death a Norman was appointed, **Turold**, of Fescamp (1069-1098); but "he neither loved his monastery, nor his convent him." During the interval between Brando's death and Turold's arrival, a partial destruction of the monastery took place. This has been already described. Some account for Hereward's share in the attack and in the carrying off of the treasures by supposing that he meant to restore them when the rule of the Norman Abbot came to an end. When Turold arrived at Peterborough he brought with him a force of 160 well-armed Normans. Joining the forces of Ivo Taillebois he attacked the Camp of Refuge near Ely. The attacking party was repulsed by Hereward, and Turold taken prisoner, and only liberated upon paying a heavy ransom. Soon afterwards the Abbot is said to have received into the monastery two monks from beyond sea, "who secretly stole away, and carried many of the Church Goods with them." At length he was made Bishop in France, and the monastery trusted they had seen the last of him. But he was ignominiously expelled in four days, and was permitted, upon paying a large sum of money to the king, to resume his abbacy.

Another uncle of Hereward's, **Godric** (1099–1103), brother

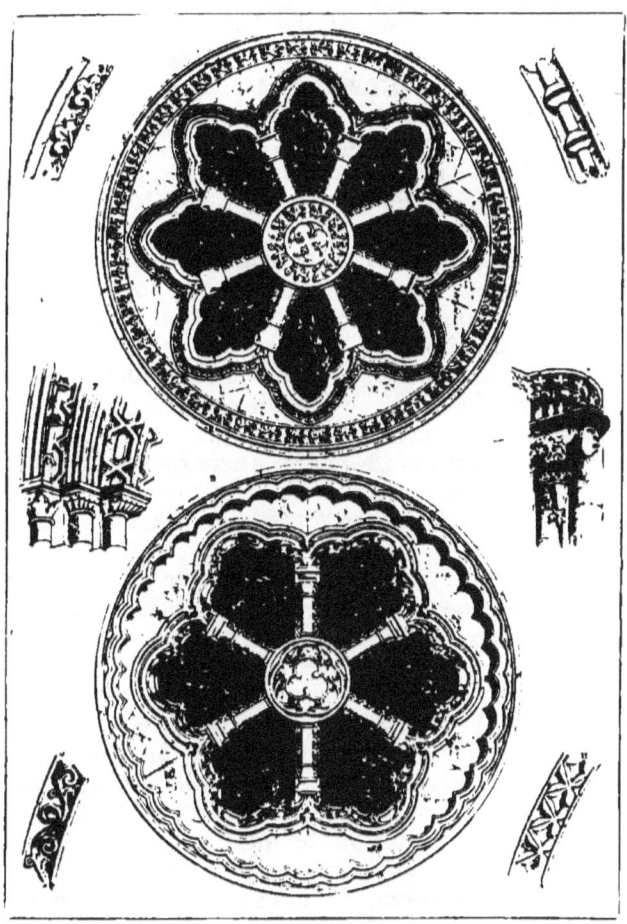

ROSE WINDOWS AND DETAILS OF WEST FRONT (BRITTON).

of Brando, became the next abbot. The monks had purchased from the king the right to elect their own abbot; and Godric, being considered by this transaction to have committed simony, was (with the neighbouring abbots of Ely and Ramsey) deposed by a council held under the presidency of Archbishop Anselm.

Matthias (1103-1105), was brother of Geoffrey, the Chief Justice, who was drowned at the foundering of The White Ship, when Prince William, the King's son, was lost. After the death of Matthias there was a vacancy of three years, until **Ernulf** (1107-1114), Prior of Canterbury came. He became Bishop of Rochester, and died in 1124.

John de Sais (1114-1125), probably came from Sez, in Normandy; though he is sometimes called John of Salisbury. In 1116 nearly the whole town was consumed by a fire that lasted nine days. It began in the bakehouse of the monastery and completely destroyed the church and most of the abbey buildings, the Chapter House, Refectory and Dormitory alone escaping. In March 1118 (or, as then written, 1117), the commencement was made of the building that now exists. Abbot John died in 1125; and again the King kept the abbey in his own hands for more than two years.

Henry of Anjou (1128-1133), where he was Abbot, was a kinsman of the King. He had numerous preferments abroad; and after five years here was forced to resign and to betake himself to Anjou.

Martin de Vecti (1133-1155), had been Prior of S. Neots. Gunton considers he came originally from the Isle of Wight, Vectis; Dean Patrick thinks he derived his name from Bec, in Normandy. He was a great builder, and was very industrious in repairing the abbey, and especially the church.

William of Waterville (1155-1175), was chaplain to King Henry II. He devoted himself to the building of the church, and the portion attributed to him has been indicated in a previous chapter. He was also very attentive to the management of the estates of the monastery, and to acquiring new ones; but his business capacity seems to have brought him into some disrepute and to have raised some enemies, who accused him to the King; and by the King's order he was deposed in the Chapter-house, as Dean Patrick relates[1] "before a multitude of abbots and monks; being neither convicted of any crime, nor confessing any, but privily accused to the Archbishop by some monks." It is recorded that he appealed to

[1] Patrick, p. 284.

the Pope against the sentence of deprivation, but without success.

Benedict (1177–1193), was Prior of Canterbury; and, towards the end of his life, Keeper of the Great Seal. He had a heavy task at the beginning of his rule in restoring discipline, which had become lax, and in reforming many evil customs that had crept into the house. He was an author, and produced a work on the career of S. Thomas of Canterbury, whose murder had taken place only seven years before Benedict came to Peterborough. He gave many ornaments and vestments to the church, and brought several relics; and in particular some of Thomas à Becket (and those we can certainly believe were more authentic than most relics), among which are mentioned his shirt and surplice, a great quantity of his blood in two crystal vessels, and two altars of the stone on which he fell when he was murdered. He was, as might be expected, very zealous in completing the chapel at the monastery gate which his predecessor had begun to raise in honour of the martyred Archbishop. Dean Stanley[1] speaks of Benedict's acquisition of the relics as "one of two memorable acts of plunder . . . curiously illustrative of the prevalent passion for such objects." He says Benedict was probably the most distinguished monk of Christ Church, and after his appointment to Peterborough, "finding that great establishment almost entirely destitute of relics, he returned to his own cathedral, and carried off with him the flagstones immediately surrounding the sacred spot, with which he formed two altars in the conventual church of his new appointment, besides two vases of blood and part of Becket's clothing." Benedict, though a member of the house and probably within the precincts, was not actually present at the Archbishop's murder. Besides his building operations (he built nearly all the nave of the church) he was very attentive to the landed property of the house, successfully recovering some estates which had been alienated.

Andrew (1193–1201) had been Prior. He was "very mild and peaceable, and made it his endeavour to plant and establish peace and tranquillity in his flock." Several fresh acquisitions of land were made in his time, and the monastery was very flourishing.

[1] Historical Memorials of Canterbury, p. 184.

Acharius (1201–1214) came here from S. Albans, where he was Prior. He devoted himself entirely to the administration of his office, managing the affairs of the monastery with the greatest care and judgement. He left behind him a reputation for "order, honesty, kindness and bounty, that from him posterity might learn how to behave themselves both in the cloister and in the world."

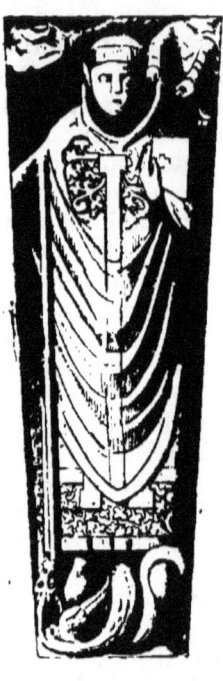

TOMB OF ABBOT ANDREW (A.D. 1201) IN SOUTH CHOIR AISLE. DRAWN BY W. H. LORD.

Robert of Lindsey (1214–1222) succeeded. This was four years after the death of his predecessor, during which period King John had kept the monastery in his own hands. This expression, which is of frequent occurrence, must be understood to mean that the king took possession of all the revenues belonging to the Abbot, and probably much more from the property of the monastery, the expenses of which would be materially lessened by the mere fact of there being no Abbot. Robert had been Sacrist here, and when he was advanced to the highest office he effected many improvements in the furniture and ornaments of the church, and in the buildings, not only of the monastery itself, but also of the manors and farms belonging to it. One alteration he effected is worth special mention; many of the windows of the church previously stuffed with reeds and straw, were glazed. The civil wars in this reign brought desolation to many religious houses: but we do not read that Peterborough suffered. Robert is said to have written a history of the monastery. He died in 1222. He had attended the fourth Lateran Council at Rome, in 1215; and had fought in person for King Henry III. at Rockingham.

Alexander of Holderness (1222–1226), the Prior, was next appointed. Dean Patrick gives, from Swapham, an account of a noteworthy agreement that was made for mutual benefit between this Abbot and the Abbot of S. Edmunds Bury. The convents "by this league were tied in a bond of special affection, for mutual counsel and assistance for ever. They were so linkt together, as to account themselves one and the same convent: so that if one of the abbots died, the survivor being desired was immediately to go to his convent; and there before him they were to make a canonical election; or if already made, they were to declare it in his presence. If the friars of either place were by any necessity driven from their monastery, the other was to receive them, and afford them a familiar refuge and aid: with a place in their Quire Chapterhouse and Refectory, *secundum conversionis suae tempus.*" This abbot is said to have been much beloved by the monks. He died in 1226.

Martin of Ramsey (1226–1233), one of the monks, was chosen to succeed Alexander. He remained only six years. After his death another monk, **Walter of S. Edmunds** (1233–1245), was elected. He was a great builder. It was during his time that the minster was solemnly re-dedicated. This abbot made no less than three visits to Rome. On the third occasion he was summoned in consequence of some irregularity in an appointment to the living of Castor; but he seems to have managed his case very adroitly, and to have escaped all censure by assigning an annuity of £10 a year to the Pope's nephew. Another account, however, represents the abbot as being so distressed at the indignities he suffered at the Papal Court, that, being unwell before he went there and his infirmities being increased by his journey, he died very soon after his return to England. "He left the abbey abounding in all good things; stored with horses, oxen, sheep and all cattle in great multitudes, and corn in some places for three years." He died in 1245.

William de Hotot (1246–1249), another monk of the house, succeeded Walter. He held the office only three years, when he resigned and was assigned a residence at the manor of Cottingham, afterwards exchanged for one at Oxney, a few miles only from Peterborough. It is said that his resignation was caused by complaints being made of his enriching his own kinsfolk, "whereof he had great multitudes swarming about him," at the expense of the monastery. But the injury he did could not have been very considerable, for his body was brought to Peterborough to be buried, and he had an honourable commemoration in the Church's calendar.

John de Caleto (1249–1262), that is, of Calais, came here from Winchester, where he was prior. He was related to the queen. As one of the Chief Justices he went on circuit. But he seems to have taken the side of the Barons in the civil war, and is said to have held the office of treasurer to them for the last two years of his life. He was seldom in residence at Peterborough, but appointed a very efficient deputy, who afterwards succeeded him as abbot.

Robert of Sutton (1262 1274) fought in the battle of Northampton against the king. The king, coming to assault the town, "espied amongst his enemies' ensigns on the wall the ensign of the Abbey of Peterburgh, whereat he was so angry that he vowed to destroy the nest of such ill birds. But the town of Northampton being reduced, Abbot Robert, by mediation of friends to the king, saved both himself and church, but was forced to pay for his delinquency, to the king 300 marks, to the queen £20, to Prince Edward £60, to the Lord Souch £6, 13s. 4d." When the fortune of war changed and the Barons were victorious at Lewes, "then did the other side fleece the Abbot of Peterburgh for his contribution to the king." After Evesham again the king repeated his exactions, and the unfortunate abbot had to pay enormously. The total amount that he paid on these several occasions is put down at a sum which seems almost impossible, being upwards of £4320. This abbot attended the Council of Lyons in 1273, and died abroad as he was returning to England. He was buried abroad; his heart, being brought to Peterborough, was interred before the altar in one of the chapels in the south transept.

Richard of London (1274–1295) is said to have been born in the parish of S. Pancras. He was a monk of the house, and while sacrist had erected the Bell-tower and given two bells. A great deal of litigation was carried on in his time, and he and the abbey were fortunate in having in one of the monks, William of Woodford, a man of great skill and judgement, to conduct the different cases before the courts. So uniformly successful was he and so wisely did he act as coadjutor of Richard when he became very old and infirm, that he was elected to the abbacy on the death of Richard of London in 1295.

William of Woodford (1295-1299) only lived four years after he became abbot. After him came **Godfrey of Crowland** (1299-1321), the celerarius of the monastery. He

IRON RAILINGS. DRAWN BY O. R. ALLBROW.

is very highly praised in the chronicles for the various services he rendered to the abbey. More than once he was at the heavy charge of entertaining the king and his court, and he contributed largely to the expenses of the war with Scotland.

Adam of Boothby (1321-1338), one of the monks, was a man of great "innocence and simplicity." His revenues were much employed in contributions to the king's expenses and in royal entertainments; and his energies devoted to divers legal difficulties connected with manors, wardships, repairs of bridges, rights of hunting, and the like. Of the last eleven abbots, whose rule extended over a period of 124 years, all but one had been monks of the place.

Henry of Morcot (1338–1353) in all probability was also one of the monks, but this is not so recorded. And the same may be said of all the remaining abbots, but the historians do not say so until the time of William in 1471. At the same time it is never said that any of them came from elsewhere.

Robert of Ramsey (1353–1361) ruled for eight years, and nothing else is known about him.

Henry of Overton (1361–1391) was abbot during the commotions in King Richard II.'s reign. The tenants with others rose up against the abbey, intending to destroy it. The Bishop of Norwich "coming to the assistance of the monastery with a strong power, forced the villains to desist from their enterprise: nay, dispersed them, and took some of them, and killed others; the rest, taking the church for sanctuary, which they intended to have destroyed, were there run through with lances and swords; some of them hard by the altar, others by the walls of the church, both within and without."

Nicholas (1391–1396), **William Genge** (1396–1408) the first mitred abbot, **John Deeping** (1408–1438) in turn succeeded. Nothing remarkable is told of them. The name of the last and the names of the next two are really the names of places; but the prefix "de" seems now to have been discontinued, and the place-name to have become a surname. Abbot John resigned his office the year before he died.

Richard Ashton (1438–1471) took great pains about the regulation of the services in the church, and drew up a customary out of the ancient usages of the place.

William Ramsey (1471–1496) appears to have devoted his time to the management of the estates and to upholding the territorial privileges of the house. If the epitaph formerly to be seen on a brass on his tomb is to be believed, he was a man prudent, just, pious, esteemed by all, chaste, kind, and adorned with every virtue.

Robert Kirton (1496–1528) has left several proofs of his energy in building, signing, as it were, the stones with his autograph. His rebus, a kirk on a ton, sometimes accompanied by the initial of his Christian name, is to be seen in the New Building, which he completed, on the Deanery gateway, and on the graceful oriel window in the Bishop's Palace. The chamber to which this window gives light still retains the name originally given of "Heaven's Gate Chamber." Much other work done by him towards the beautifying of the church and buildings has perished.

The last abbot was **John Chambers** (1528–1540). One incident of considerable interest is related as having taken place in his first year. "Cardinal Wolsey came to Peterburgh, where he kept his Easter. Upon Palm Sunday he carried his palm, going with the monks in procession, and the Thursday following he kept his Maundy, washing and kissing the feet of fifty-nine poor people, and having dried them, he gave to every one of them 12d. and three ells of canvas for a shirt; he gave also to each of them a pair of shoes and a portion of red herrings. On Easter day he went in procession in his cardinal's vestments, and sang the High-Mass himself after a solemn manner, which he concluded with his benediction and remission upon all the hearers." This abbot was a native of Peterborough, and was sometimes known as John Burgh; and on the brass placed on his tomb he was called "Johannes Burgh, Burgo natus." A monumental effigy was also erected to him, "made of white chalkstone"; and this is almost certainly the figure now placed (temporarily) at the back of the apse. This abbot was B.D. of Cambridge and one of the king's chaplains. It was during his time that Queen Katherine of Arragon was interred in the minster. The well-known story that the building was spared by the king out of regard to the memory of his first wife is told by Dean Patrick in these words:—[1]"There is this traditional story goes concerning the preservation of this church at the dissolution of abbeys: that a little after Queen Katherine's interment here (which Mr G. mentions), some courtiers suggesting to the king how well it would become his greatness to erect a fair monument for her, he answered, 'Yes, he would leave her one of the goodliest monuments in Christendom,' meaning this church, for he had then in his thoughts the demolishing of abbeys, which shortly after followed." Abbot Chambers surrendered

[1] Patrick, p. 330.

the monastery to the king in 1540, and was appointed guardian of the temporalities, with a pension of £266, 13s. 4d. and 100 loads of wood. The king divided the whole property of the abbey into three parts, retaining one-third for himself, and assigning the other parts upon the foundation of the see to the Bishop and Chapter respectively. If the annual value of the portion he reserved for his own use may be taken to be exactly one-third of the possessions of the abbey, the entire property must have been worth as nearly as possible £2200 per annum. The last abbot became the first bishop.

It is remarkable that of the two queens buried at Peterborough, the body of one has been removed to Westminster by the orders of her son, and that a similar removal had been previously designed for the body of the other. Queen Katherine's daughter, Queen Mary, left directions in her will that "the body of the virtuous Lady and my most dere and well-beloved mother of happy memory, Queen Kateryn, which lyeth now buried at Peterborowh," should be removed and laid near the place of her own sepulture, and that honourable monuments should be made for both. It would have been a singular coincidence if this intention had been carried out.

CHAPTER VI.

HISTORY OF THE DIOCESE.

THE Abbey Church was converted into the Cathedral of the newly-founded diocese of Peterborough by deed bearing date September 4, 1541. The counties of Northampton and Rutland were the limits of the new see. The king's original plan for the establishment of bishoprics out of the confiscated estates of monastic establishments was too generous to be put into practice. He designed the foundation of no less than twenty-one new sees. In this scheme Northamptonshire and Huntingdonshire were assigned to the diocese of Peterborough; and, considering the situation of the new cathedral, this would have been a more satisfactory arrangement than the one which was ultimately carried out. The only change that has been made in the limits of the diocese is that, in the year 1839, the county of Leicester was detached from the see of Lincoln and joined to Peterborough.

As has been said above, the first bishop was **John Chambers** (1541–1556). He was consecrated[1] in the minster on the 23rd of October 1541, by Thomas (Thirlby), Bishop of Ely, Robert (Blyth), Bishop of Down, last Abbot of Thorney, Suffragan of Ely, and Thomas (Hallam or Swillington), Bishop of Philadelphia, Suffragan of Lincoln. Strype has an account of his costly funeral. The two memorials to him in the church had been erected by himself in his lifetime.

David Pole (1556–1559) is generally held to have been a relative (some say a nephew) of Cardinal Reginald Pole. He was Dean of the Arches. He was not consecrated till August 1557, and so held the bishopric less than two years, being deprived by Queen Elizabeth in June 1559. He lived quietly in London till his death in 1568.

---

[1] Stubbs' *Episcopal Succession*, p. 79.

Edmund Scambler (1560–1584) in the Roman index of books prohibited is called Pseudo-Episcopus, no doubt because there was another Bishop of Peterborough, Pole, still living. He alienated many of the lands and manors of his bishopric to the queen and to her courtiers; and as a reward he was translated to Norwich, where he died ten years later.

Richard Howland (1584–1600) was Master of Magdalene, and afterwards of S. John's, Cambridge. He was present at the funeral of Mary Queen of Scots. He was buried at the upper end of the choir, but no stone or monument exists to his memory.

Thomas Dove (1600–1630) was Dean of Norwich. He was[1] "a lover of hospitality, keeping a very free house, and having always a numerous family, yet was so careful of posterity that he left a fair estate to his heirs." He was buried in the north transept. "Over his body was erected a very comely monument of long quadrangular form, having four corner pilasters supporting a fair table of black marble, and, within, the pourtraiture of the bishop lying in his Episcopal habit." This was destroyed in 1643. There was a long Latin inscription in prose and verse, and among the verses these occur:—

> "Hoc addam: Hic illa est senio argentata Columba
> Davidis, cœlos hinc petit ille suos."

This monument was erected by the bishop's eldest son, Sir William Dove, Kt., of Upton.

William Peirse (1630–1632) was promoted from the Deanery. He only remained here as bishop two years, when he was translated to Bath and Wells. "A man of excellent parts, both in divinity and knowledge of the laws: very vigilant and active he was for the good both of the ecclesiastical and civil state." He was silenced during the civil war, but restored in 1660. On his tombstone, at Walthamstow, it is said "*Templum Cathedrale Wellense reparavit, Episcopale Palatium exædificavit, cœlis maturus terris valedixit an. æt. 94 salut. 1670.*"

Augustine Lindsell (1632–1634) was Dean of Lichfield. He was translated to Hereford after being bishop here two years, but died within a few months.

Francis Dee (1634–1638) was Dean of Chichester. "He was a man of very pious life and affable behaviour." He

---
[1] Gunton, p. 82.

founded scholarships and fellowships at S. John's College, Cambridge, of which he had been Fellow, for boys from the King's School, Peterborough, of his name or kindred. In 1637 Archbishop Laud reported to the King that "My Lord of Peterborough hath taken a great deal of pains and brought his diocese into very good order." He left by will £100 to the repairs of the Cathedral, and the same amount to the repairs of S. Paul's. He was buried in the choir, near the throne.

John Towers (1638-1649) was one of the King's chaplains. He was promoted from the Deanery. He protested, with eleven other bishops, against the opposition that was made by the Parliamentary party to their taking their seats in the House of Lords, in which protest it was declared that all laws, orders, votes, or resolutions, were in themselves null and of none effect, which in their absence from Dec. 27th 1641, had been passed, or should afterwards be passed, during the time of their enforced absence. For this they were committed to the Tower, and kept there four or five months. Being set free he was allowed to return to Peterborough, but his revenues were taken away. Living here in a state of continual alarm, he betook himself to the king's forces at Oxford, where he remained until the surrender of the place. Coming back here in 1646 his health failed, and he died about three weeks before the king was beheaded. He was buried in the choir.

DETAILS OF CHASUBLE ON EFFIGY IN SOUTH CHOIR AISLE.

No successor was appointed until the Restoration. **Benjamin Laney** (1660-1663) was then made Bishop. He was Dean of Rochester, and had been Master of Pembroke, Cambridge. He was translated to Lincoln in 1663, and to Ely in 1667. He died in 1675, and is buried at Lambeth.

Joseph Henshaw (1663-1679) was Dean of Chichester. He died suddenly on March 9, 1679, on his return from attending service at Westminster Abbey. He was buried at East Lavant in Sussex, where he had been rector.

William Lloyd (1679 1685) was translated from Llandaff, and was further translated to Norwich in 1685. He was deprived of his see as a Nonjuror in 1691. He lived at Hammersmith till his death in 1710. He was the last survivor of the seven deprived bishops. It is singular that his namesake, William Lloyd, bishop of S. Asaph, should have been one of the seven bishops committed to the Tower by King James II. in 1688 ; but he had no scruples about taking the oaths to the new sovereigns, and became afterwards Bishop of Lichfield, and ultimately of Worcester.

Thomas White (1685-1691) was one of the seven committed to the Tower, and also one of the seven deprived in 1691 as Nonjurors. He attended Sir John Fenwick on the scaffold. This bishop, with his predecessor, Bishop Lloyd, the deprived Bishop of Norwich, were two of the consecrators of the Nonjuring Bishops, Hickes and Wagstaffe. There were really ten bishops (including Archbishop Sancroft) who refused the oaths to William and Mary ; but the Bishops of Worcester, Chichester, and Chester died before the time fixed for the deprivation. Bishop White lived in retirement after he left his diocese. He died in 1698, and his funeral is mentioned in Evelyn's *Diary*, under date June 5th : " Dr White, late Bishop of Peterborough, who had been deprived for not complying with Government, was buried in St Gregory's churchyard or vault, at St Paul's. His hearse was accompanied by two Nonjuror bishops, Dr Turner of Ely, and Dr Lloyd, with forty Nonjuror clergymen, who could not stay the office of the burial, because the Dean of St Paul's had appointed a conforming minister to read the office, at which all much wondered, there being nothing in that office which mentioned the present king." Lathbury remarks on this retirement from the grave, that it was a singular circumstance, and contrary to the practice of the Nonjurors in many other cases.

Richard Cumberland (1691-1718) had a reputation as a philosophical writer. The only memoir of him is to be found in the preface to *Sanchoniathon's History*,[1] a posthumous work, in which his chaplain (and son-in-law) thus describes his

---

[1] P. 12 ; quoted in the account of Bishop Cumberland in the *Penny Cyclopædia*, viii. 229.

appointment: — "The king was told that Dr Cumberland was the fittest man he could nominate to the bishopric of Peterborough. Thus a private country clergyman, without posting to Court—a place he had rarely seen— without suing to great men, without taking the least step towards soliciting for it, was pitched upon to fill a great trust, only because he was fittest for it. He walked after his usual manner on a post-day to the coffee-house, and read in the newspaper that one Dr Cumberland of Stamford was named to the bishopric of Peterborough, a greater surprise to himself than to anybody else." His chaplain speaks of the bishop's character, zeal, and learning in terms of unqualified praise. One of the bishop's sons, Richard, was Archdeacon of Northampton, and father of Denison Cumberland, Bishop of Clonfert and of Kilmore. This last named married a daughter of Dr Bentley, the famous Master of Trinity College, Cambridge, and one of their sons was Richard Cumberland, the dramatist. Bishop Richard Cumberland is buried in the Cathedral, and a tablet to his memory remains in the New Building.

White Kennett (1718-1728) had been Dean. He was a most industrious writer, many of his works, which are upwards of fifty in number, being most laborious. His manuscript collections in the British Museum are also of great value. He is best known from his antiquarian tastes and studies, and for having directed the attention of his clergy to the value of parish registers. It would seem that before his time no transcripts of parish registers were ever sent to the Bishop's Registry at Peterborough. The earliest transcripts now to be found date only from the beginning of his episcopate, except that, in a few instances, some incumbents appear to have sent the entries for six or eight years previously. Notwithstanding the efficiency of his predecessor he "found the irregularities of the diocese great and many." The Cathedral service was negligently conducted, many clergy were non-resident, some small benefices had been left unfilled. Many other abuses were discovered from time to time. Bishop Kennett was most active and conscientious in administering his office, and thoroughly re-organised the diocese; but his strong political partisanship made for him a great number of enemies. The enmity he raised came to a culminating point while he was still dean. An altar-piece representing the Last Supper had been painted for Whitechapel Church.[1] In this Judas was painted turning round to the spectator, and was intended to represent Kennett. We do not know whether the likeness in itself was sufficiently good to be recognised, but the intention was sufficiently indicated by a black patch in the centre of the forehead, just under the wig. Kennett always wore such a patch, to hide a scar which had remained after being trepanned in early manhood. Judas is, moreover, represented as cleanshaven, being the only figure so drawn except the Evangelist S. John. Great scandal and excitement were caused by this picture, and it was removed. It ultimately found a home at S. Albans Abbey, where it may still be seen (patch and all), but no longer in the position it once occupied over the high altar. Bishop Kennett died in 1728, and is buried in the New Building.

Robert Clavering (1728–1747) was consecrated Bishop of Llandaff in 1725, and translated to Peterborough in 1728. He is buried here, but no memorial exists.

John Thomas (1747–1757) was Canon of S. Paul's. He was translated to Sarum in 1757, and to Winchester in 1761. He was preceptor to Prince George, afterwards King George III., who used to visit him at Farnham Castle. In the early part of his episcopate he had a namesake on the bench, John Thomas, formerly Dean of Peterborough, who was made Bishop of Lincoln in 1744, and of Sarum in 1761; and during the latter part another namesake, John Thomas, Bishop of Rochester from 1775 to 1793. Bishop Thomas of Winchester died in 1781, in his 85th year, and is buried in his cathedral.

Richard Terrick (1757–1764) was Canon of S. Paul's. He was translated to London in 1764, and died in 1777.

Robert Lamb (1764–1769) had been Dean. He is buried at Hatfield, where he had been rector.

John Hinchcliffe (1769–1794) is an instance of a man, rising from an inferior station to positions of the greatest eminence. His father was a stable-master in London. Proceeding from Westminster School to Trinity College, Cambridge, he obtained a Fellowship there. He afterwards, through a gentleman of wealth to whom he was tutor, secured some very

---

[1] A full account of this famous picture with an engraving is given in *Northamptonshire Notes and Queries*, iv. 209.

influential friends, and became Head Master of Westminster School, Chaplain to the King, and Master of Trinity. This last appointment he continued to hold with his bishopric until 1789, when he was made Dean of Durham. A memoir published at the time of his death describes him as learned, assiduous in his duties, obliging in his manners, and honest and sincere in his religious and political principles. He died in 1794, and is buried in the cathedral.

Spencer Madan (1794-1813) was a prebendary and king's chaplain, and first cousin to the poet Cowper. He

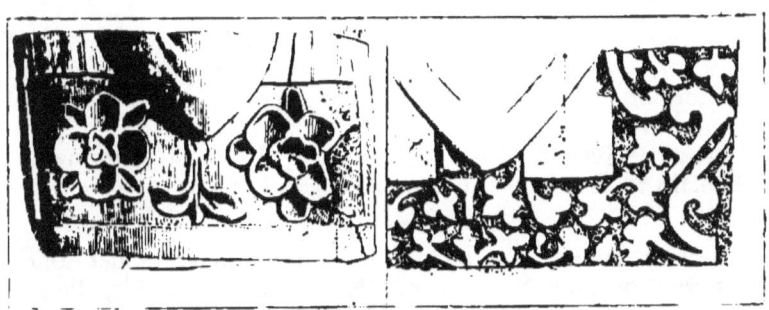

DETAILS OF OF CHASUBLES ON EFFIGIES IN CHOIR AISLES.

came back to Peterborough from Bristol, to which see he was consecrated in 1792. He is buried in the New Building.

John Parsons (1813-1819) was Master of Balliol and Dean of Bristol. He was a man of great mark and influence at Oxford, where he died and was buried. There is a monument to him in the chapel of Balliol.

Herbert Marsh (1819-1839) was the author of many controversial works. He was translated to this see from Llandaff, where he had been bishop since 1816. He was buried in the New Building—the last bishop interred in the cathedral.

George Davys (1839-1864) was Dean of Chester, and had been preceptor to Queen Victoria. He was buried in the Cathedral Yard; the Queen sent one of her carriages with servants in state liveries to attend the funeral as a mark of her affection and esteem.

Francis Jeune (1864-1868) had been Dean of Jersey, Master of Pembroke, Oxford, and Dean of Lincoln. His eldest son is now the well-known judge. Bishop Jeune is buried in the Cathedral Yard.

William Connor Magee (1868-1891) was Dean of Cork. He was translated to the Archbishopric of York, but died within a very few months, May 5th, 1891. He is buried in the Cathedral Yard, where a massive cross of Irish marble has been erected over his grave. In the south choir aisle of the cathedral there is also a recumbent effigy, the likeness to the deceased prelate being most remarkably good. His career is so recent and his eminence so well known that it is unnecessary to speak of them.

Mandell Creighton (1891-1897) had been Canon of Windsor, and previously of Worcester. He was translated to London when Bishop Temple became Archbishop of Canterbury.

Hon. Edward Carr Glyn (1897) Vicar of Kensington, Chaplain to the Queen, is the present bishop.

Without giving a list of all the Deans, it may be mentioned that four became Bishops of Peterborough, namely, Peirse, Towers, Kennett, and Lamb; John Boxall was also Dean of Norwich and of Windsor; Richard Fletcher was successively Bishop of Bristol, Worcester, and London; George Meriton was removed to the Deanery of York; Thomas Nevill became Dean of Canterbury; William Gee was removed to the Deanery of Lincoln; Henry Beaumont was Dean of Windsor; John Cosin became Bishop of Durham at the restoration of King Charles II.; Edward Rainbow became Bishop of Carlisle; Simon Patrick was made Bishop of Chichester, and afterwards of Ely; Richard Kidder became Bishop of Bath and Wells; Richard Reynolds was Bishop of Bangor, and then of Lincoln; John Thomas was Bishop of Lincoln, and then of Sarum; Charles Manners Sutton became Bishop of Norwich and Dean of Windsor, and ultimately Archbishop of Canterbury; James Henry Monk became Bishop of Gloucester and Bristol; Thomas Turton, Dean of Westminster and Bishop of Ely; and, lastly, John James Stewart Perowne is the present Bishop of Worcester. There have been in all, thirty-eight deans and of these no less than fifteen have become bishops.

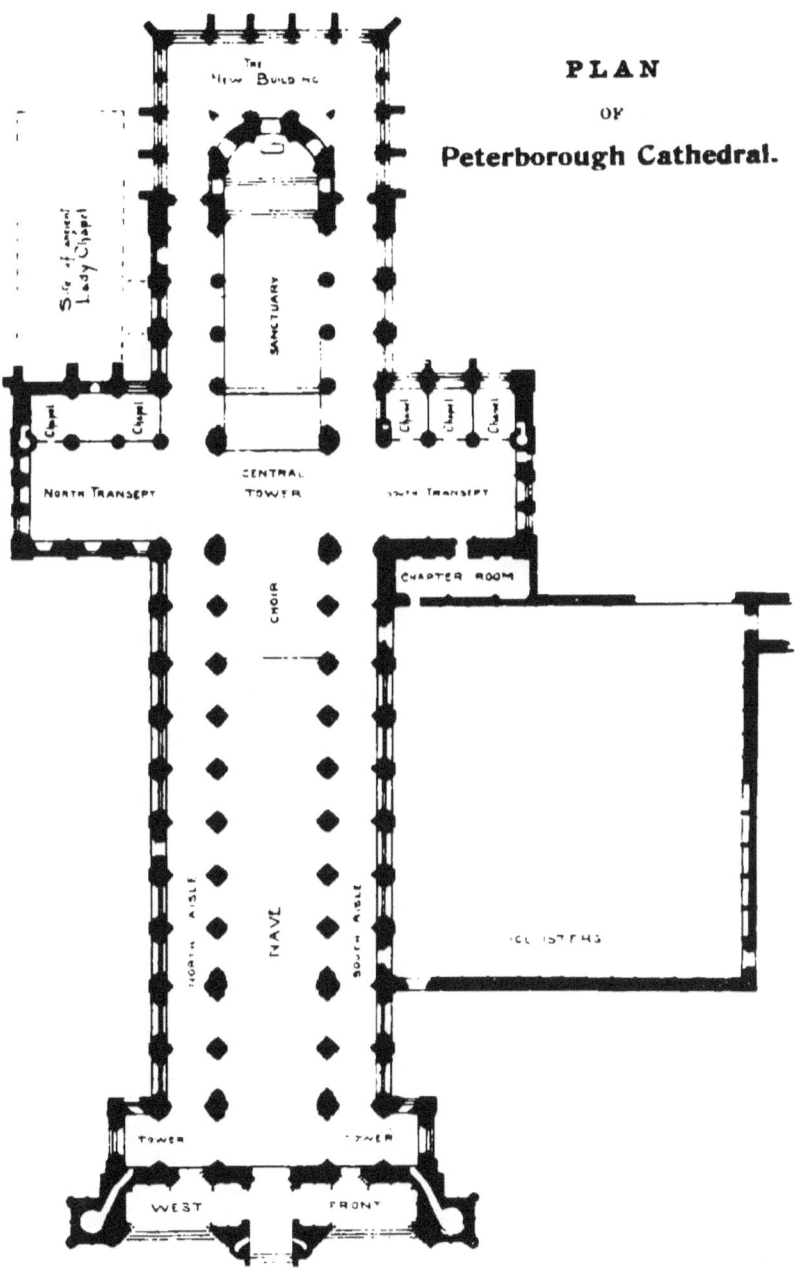

Bell's Cathedral Series.

EDITED BY

GLEESON WHITE AND E. F. STRANGE.

In specially designed cloth cover, crown 8vo, 1s. 6d. each.

Now Ready.

CANTERBURY. By HARTLEY WITHERS. 2nd Edition, revised. 36 Illustrations.
SALISBURY. By GLEESON WHITE. 2nd Edition, revised. 50 Illustrations.
CHESTER. By CHARLES HIATT. 24 Illustrations.
ROCHESTER. By G. H. PALMER, B.A. 38 Illustrations.
OXFORD. By Rev. PERCY DEARMER, M.A. 34 Illustrations.
EXETER. By PERCY ADDLESHAW, B.A. 35 Illustrations.
PETERBOROUGH. By Rev. W. D. SWEETING. 51 Illustrations.
WINCHESTER. By P. W. SERGEANT. 50 Illustrations.
NORWICH. By C. H. B. QUENNELL. 38 Illustrations.
LICHFIELD. By A. B. CLIFTON. 42 Illustrations.
HEREFORD. By A. HUGH FISHER. 34 Illustrations.

Preparing.

LINCOLN. By A. B. KENDRICK, B.A.
DURHAM. By J. E. BYGATE.
WELLS. By Rev. PERCY DEARMER, M.A.
ST DAVID'S. By PHILIP ROBSON.
CHICHESTER. CARLISLE.
ST ALBANS. ST PAUL'S.

SOUTHWELL. By Rev. ARTHUR DIMOCK.
ELY. By T. D. ATKINSON.
WORCESTER. By E. F. STRANGE.
YORK. By A. CLUTTON BROCK, B.A.
BRISTOL. GLOUCESTER.
RIPON.

Uniform with the above Series.

BEVERLEY MINSTER. By CHARLES HIATT. [*Preparing.*

Opinions of the Press.

"For the purpose at which they aim they are admirably done, and there are few visitants to any of our noble shrines who will not enjoy their visit the better for being furnished with one of these delightful books, which can be slipped into the pocket and carried with ease, and is yet distinct and legible. . . . A volume such as that on Canterbury is exactly what we want, and on our next visit we hope to have it with us. It is thoroughly helpful, and the views of the fair city and its noble cathedral are beautiful. Both volumes, moreover, will serve more than a temporary purpose, and are trustworthy as well as delightful."—*Notes and Queries.*

"We have so frequently in these columns urged the want of cheap, well-illustrated, and well-written handbooks to our cathedrals, to take the place of the out-of-date publications of local booksellers, that we are glad to hear that they have been taken in hand by Messrs George Bell and Sons."—*St James's Gazette.*

"Visitors to the cathedral cities of England must often have felt the need of some work dealing with the history and antiquities of the city itself, and the architecture and associations of the cathedral, more portable than the elaborate monographs which have been devoted to some of them, more scholarly and satisfying than the average local guide-book, and more copious than the section devoted to them in the general guide-book of the county or district. Such a legitimate need the 'Cathedral Series' now being issued by Messrs George Bell & Sons, under the editorship of Mr Gleeson White and Mr E. F. Strange, seems well calculated to supply. The volumes are handy in size, moderate in price, well illustrated, and written in a scholarly spirit. The history of cathedral and city is intelligently set forth and accompanied by a descriptive survey of the building in all its detail. The illustrations are copious and well selected, and the series bids fair to become an indispensable companion to the cathedral tourist in England."—*Times.*

"They are nicely produced in good type, on good paper, and contain numerous illustrations, are well written, and very cheap. We should imagine architects and students of architecture will be sure to buy the series as they appear, for they contain in brief much valuable information."—*British Architect.*

"Half the charm of this little book on Canterbury springs from the writer's recognition of the historical association of so majestic a building with the fortunes, destinies, and habits of the English people. . . . One admirable feature of the book is its artistic illustrations. They are both lavish and satisfactory—even when regarded with critical eyes."—*Speaker.*

"Every aspect of Salisbury is passed in swift, picturesque survey in this charming little volume, and the illustrations in this case also heighten perceptibly the romantic appeal of an unconventional but scholarly guide-book."—*Speaker.*

"There is likely to be a large demand for these attractive handbooks."—*Globe.*

"Bell's 'Cathedral Series,' so admirably edited, is more than a description of the various English cathedrals. It will be a valuable historical record, and a work of much service also to the architect. The illustrations are well selected, and in many cases not mere bald architectural drawings but reproductions of exquisite stone fancies, touched in their treatment by fancy and guided by art."—*Star.*

"Each of them contains exactly that amount of information which the intelligent visitor, who is not a specialist, will wish to have. The disposition of the various parts is judiciously proportioned, and the style is very readable. The illustrations supply a further important feature; they are both numerous and good. A series which cannot fail to be welcomed by all who are interested in the ecclesiastical buildings of England."—*Glasgow Herald.*

"Those who, either for purposes of professional study or for a cultured recreation, find it expedient to 'do' the English cathedrals will welcome the beginning of Bell's 'Cathedral Series.' This set of books is an attempt to consult, more closely, and in greater detail than the usual guide-books do, the needs of visitors to the cathedral towns. The series cannot but prove markedly successful. In each book a business-like description is given of the fabric of the church to which the volume relates, and an interesting history of the relative diocese. The books are plentifully illustrated, and are thus made attractive as well as instructive. They cannot but prove welcome to all classes of readers interested either in English Church history or in ecclesiastical architecture."—*Scotsman.*

"A set of little books which may be described as very useful, very pretty, and very cheap . . . . and alike in the letterpress, the illustrations, and the remarkably choice binding, they are ideal guides."—*Liverpool Daily Post.*

"They have nothing in common with the almost invariably wretched local guides save portability, and their only competitors in the quality and quantity of their contents are very expensive and mostly rare works, each of a size that suggests a packing-case rather than a coat-pocket. The 'Cathedral Series' are important compilations concerning history, architecture, and biography, and quite popular enough for such as take any sincere interest in their subjects."—*Sketch.*

LONDON : GEORGE BELL AND SONS.

www.ingramcontent.com/pod-product-compliance
Lightning Source LLC
Chambersburg PA
CBHW030356170426
43202CB00010B/1388